THE ULTIMATE WEALTH GUIDE FOR REAL ESTATE AGENTS

AND ANYONE ELSE INTERESTED IN PROPERTY INVESTMENT

MARK REISTER

Copyright 2018 © Mark Reister. All rights reserved.

No part of this book may be copied, reproduced, adapted, stored in a retrieval system, communicated or transmitted in any form or by any means without prior written permission from the author. All inquiries should be made to the author via the web address below.

This book is intended only to provide information on the subject matter covered. It is sold on the understanding that the publisher and author are not engaged in rendering professional services. If you need professional advice or other expert assistance, please seek the services of a competent and qualified professional.

ALSO BY MARK REISTER

How to Buy Unlimited Investment Properties
Buy Unlimited Properties and Retire in 10 Years
(available individually or as a 2-volume boxed set)

All profits from this book will be donated to The Fred Hollows Foundation.
Please turn to the very back of this book to find out more about the vital work The Foundation does in attempting to eradicate preventable blindness and eye diseases.

These core activities are fundamental to the success of each individual and consequently the real estate agency as a whole. So it's no surprise that these activities are closely monitored, measured, and analysed, and reported on day after day, week after week, and month after month.

Real estate agencies have a rather narrow view of what they do. In essence, they list and sell real estate, and they look after people's rental properties. A real estate business rarely looks beyond its budget and what it has to do for the present month. At the beginning of the year, the business will set a budget for the next 12 months, taking into account seasonal changes, school and public holidays, and so on. But once that 12-month budget is set, the agency's staff rarely revisit it. Instead, they steadfastly focus on the current month's budget and the tasks they need to perform to reach that figure. In an effort to reach the monthly budget, the agency micromanages every aspect of the agent's day, from the number of phone calls they make to the number of face-to-face contacts they have with clients and prospective buyers. In fact, some real estate offices will not let a sales consultant finish a day's work until they have achieved at least one desired outcome for the day, such as booking a home appraisal, listing or selling a home, or reducing the price of a home listed for sale.

At the end of every month, performances are reviewed. Top agents are rewarded. Those who aren't doing so well are monitored. But however good or bad your last month was, at the start of a new month, you start all over again, refocusing your efforts for the month ahead and not resting on your laurels. You make the calls, meet homeowners, appraise their properties, meet potential buyers or renters, prepare advertising, and prospect for new listings. You attend your weekly meetings and let your colleagues and managers know how you are performing, and hopefully at the end of the month, if everything goes to plan, you personally, and your agency, will have made budget.

As I have mentioned, every one of those activities is essential to ensuring the success of each estate agent, and of the real estate office as a whole. In this book, though, I will not discuss any of those time-honoured activities further. The real estate industry offers extensive training courses on everything I've mentioned so far, and most real estate offices have their own compulsory in-house training sessions.

If you would like to attend training courses on any of these time-tested activities, there are enough courses available to keep you in the classroom every day for the rest of your life.

This book is different.

In the pages that follow, I discuss how you, as a real estate agent or as someone interested in property investment, can make a secondary income, separate from your wage, that will give you and your family financial security and freedom for the rest of your life.

My history as an estate agent and investor

I worked in the real estate industry as a sales consultant between 1993 and 2010, and between 2010 and 2017 I was the part-owner of my own real estate agency. I have sat through countless meetings and training sessions. But it wasn't until around 2005 (12 years after starting my career in real estate) that I started thinking beyond my monthly budget and sales targets and began thinking about the larger benefits of working in the industry and investing in real estate.

Once I did, it led me to where I am now: in 2016, after

following the methods I talk about in this and my other two books (*How to Buy Unlimited Investment Properties* and *Buy Unlimited Properties and Retire in 10 Years*), I retired at the age of 46.

While I am very grateful for everything in my life and I have no regrets, I wish I had started my investment journey earlier. In all my years working in the real estate industry, no one ever asked me, "Where would you like to be a year from now, or beyond that?", "What would you like to be doing in the future?", or "What would you like to achieve?" I am not criticising the industry I love for not asking these questions; I am thankful for my career and the opportunities I've received. However, as I mentioned, the real estate industry has a narrow view of what it does and needs to do. Managers and staff micromanage every aspect of their days but do not ask the bigger questions, like where they will be in 10 years —or even in two.

I believe it is now time for the industry and estate agents to take a longer-term view of what they can achieve together for the mutual benefit of employees and agencies alike.

This book may challenge some of the conventional thinking in real estate. It may provoke a culture change. The strategies it describes require a view of what agents and agencies want to and can achieve that is broader and longer-term than we often see in the industry.

How this book works, and who it is for

The interests of agents and agencies are not mutually exclusive. What benefits one benefits the other. So regardless of where you fit within your real estate agency, you can read this book from cover to cover and find useful information throughout. But because each reader will have their own perspective and interests at the front of their mind, I have broken this book up into two parts:

1. "**The Estate Agent**" deals with the individual. It is primarily for people who work in a real estate office and earn a salary.
2. The second part, "**The Real Estate Agency**" looks at the benefits for the business and its owner(s). Business owners derive their income from the collective efforts of the people who work in the business.

If you are reading this book and you don't work in, or have any financial interest in, the real estate industry, you will still find a lot of useful information here that you can use as a property investor. You only need one good idea from a book or training course to potentially change your life. Hopefully, you will find at least one diamond here that will help you create wealth for yourself into the future. If this describes you, I believe the first part of this book, "The Estate Agent", will be most relevant to you. Among other things, it describes investment programs that real estate agents are best placed to set up for their clients, which you can benefit from equally by participating in them as an investor.

As you are reading, keep in mind one of the fundamental principles I live by, as described in my first book, *How to Buy Unlimited Investment Properties*, which is to only take advice from people who have achieved what you want to achieve. Find an estate agent who is doing the things I describe in this book, make sure they have achieved what you want to achieve, and work with that person.

Regardless of which category you fit into—estate agent, principal, or simply interested in real estate—I hope this book broadens your thinking. I would like the industry to start thinking beyond this month's budget and commission. I would like you to start thinking about next year and the years after that. As I have indicated, this may require a fundamental shift from the conventional mindset, but I wish someone had asked me these questions when I worked in real estate. If they had, I believe I would have started on my path to wealth and independence much sooner.

PART I

THE ESTATE AGENT

In my experience, the overwhelming majority of estate agents work long hours, are honest, ethical people who are eager to please, and have the best interest of their clients at heart. This is true for both selling agents and property (rental) managers. Unfortunately, the actions of a few rogue agents can spoil the reputation of the whole industry, and this small minority can, and often does, taint the public's perception of estate agents. Because real estate is so competitive and every aspect of the agent's day is micromanaged, it is essential that agents provide outstanding service to their clients.

In the case of a selling agent, everything they do aims at hopefully winning another listing or sale. It's all about making the next commission.

Likewise, most things a property manager does each day are micromanaged, but not every activity is designed to bring in a new rental property: their day is mostly spent looking after rental properties they already manage, while a small part is set aside for prospecting activities to attract new rental properties for the agency.

Regardless of whether an estate agent works in the sales or rental department, they have annual and monthly budgets that are closely monitored. A salesperson focuses on the number of sales they can make and the amount of commission they generate. A rental manager concentrates on the number of new rental properties they can bring into the real estate agency, and the fees they can charge.

A sales consultant's income is usually entirely derived from commission, whereas a property manager usually receives a set income with bonuses for new listings and the many other money-generating tasks they perform for their clients. Regardless of whether an agent works in the sales department or rental-management department, there are financial incentives for making the business money. Because of these financial incentives, estate agents are only too happy to help their clients with real estate matters, including **investing** in real estate.

Estate agents are very quick to freely give away valuable information to would-be investors, in the hope that they will make a commission or bonus, but have they ever stopped and considered what that valuable information is worth? Astute investors will frequently and openly pick the brain of the local estate agent in the area they are considering investing in. And why shouldn't they? The local agent is the area expert, and can give the investor vital information on a range of important points that are crucial as the investor determines the merits of an investment. Things the astute investor will want to know include:

- the current market value of the proposed investment property

- the median house, unit, or apartment price in the area
- the current (or anticipated) rental income for the proposed investment property
- suggestions on how to increase the rental return for the property
- suggestions on how to increase the capital growth of the property
- vacancy rates in the area
- profiles of the tenants most suited to the proposed rental property
- details about renting the property, including condition reports, bonds, insurances, ongoing fees and maintenance, and so on
- the real estate agency's management fees
- how long it will take to find a tenant
- proximity to key public amenities such as schools, shops, and public transport
- the best addresses in the area, and those that are not so desirable

The estate agent has accumulated all this information and more in the hope that one day they can impart their wisdom to a grateful investor and make a sale and commission.

The local estate agent is undeniably the most knowledgeable property expert in their area. Every day, they drive up and down the local streets. They know every property listed for sale, and every sale made in the area since they began working as an estate agent there, and usually for several years before that. They get this information from websites such as pricefinder.com and realestate.com, which show historical sales information. The local estate agent's knowledge of the area is far superior to anyone else's, including that of valuers (discussed in chapters 1 and 13 of *How to Buy Unlimited Investment Properties* and chapter 3 of *Buy Unlimited Properties and Retire in 10 Years*), because they work exclusively in the same area every day.

Every week, the estate agent scours local newspapers and the internet to see if any new properties have been listed for sale. They also keep a keen eye out for every sale made. If a property is advertised for sale in the local area but the ad only gives the suburb and not the full address, the estate agent will usually be able to tell you precisely where it is, even if it's not listed with their agency. That's because they know every street in the suburb intimately. On a regular basis, usually weekly, they drive up and down every street in their business development area (BDA, aka "farm area") taking care of things like sign control. The estate agent has most likely walked up and down every street, at least a few times during the year, to carry out prospecting activities like letter-box drops and door-knocking. These activities, and the intimate knowledge of an area that comes through them, are the bedrock of the agent's education and understanding.

It takes time to develop this level of knowledge, but gradually, day by day, the agent's knowledge of the area grows until there isn't a listing or sale made in an area without that agent knowing, even if it was made by a competing real estate agency.

When I was an estate agent, I was just like all the other agents I know: I was happy to impart all my knowledge to any would-be investor. In fact, I was delighted to help anyone thinking of investing in real estate. I had a huge breadth of knowledge, and I secretly took delight in imparting more information than other agents did. I wanted to be seen as the most knowledgeable agent in my area. It felt like a competition—even if I was the only one participating. I took great pride in telling the investor important things that no other agent had.

This served me well over the years. I was a successful agent, and many investors kept coming back to me year after year. Why wouldn't they? I would let them know what homes had sold for in the street and area, what rental properties we were managing in the close vicinity, how they could increase their rental income, what the gross and net rental returns would be (to a high degree of accuracy), how the property would be geared and what their net cash flow would be.

I would freely and openly give all this information away in the hope that the investor would buy a property from me and I would make a commission. Even if the investor did not buy an investment property from me, but from a competing real estate agency, the investor would usually give me and our agency the investment property to manage. When this happened, I still received a small bonus for bringing the rental management into our office.

Naturally, I was delighted when investors came back to me year after year to buy more investment properties. It meant I was doing my job well, investors were placing their faith in me, and, more importantly, that I would keep making more commission. Everything was working well, but here is something every person knows (or should know) about making money:

The more money you make, the more you spend.

Regardless of your age or sex, the more you make, the more you spend. When you make more money, you buy more expensive things, and more of them. You will buy more expensive suits, more expensive shoes, a more expensive watch, the latest smartphone and tablet, a later-model European car and better stationery, and that's just for work. It's in our nature. We are consumers, and it keeps the world's economy moving.

Some people are innate savers and fantastic money managers, but even they cannot deny the correlation between earning more and spending more. So, like so many before me and many that will come after, I made lots of commission and spent accordingly. Spending your hard-earned commission is a very satisfying outcome of all the hard work you have done, and it is also a status symbol. Not only do you want to *be* successful, you want to be *seen* as successful. Other people's perception of you is their reality.

It can seem that most, if not all, successful real estate agents drive a late-model European car and wear an expensive suit and designer watch, and you feel you had better do the same to fit the image of what a successful real estate agent looks like. People are attracted to successful people, and you want to keep being successful. In fact, you want to be more successful year after year, so spending money really sounds like an investment in yourself and your future success. After a while, it feels like you are running on a treadmill. You're running faster and faster, but you don't remember touching the speed control. If you don't keep up, you will fall over, and the faster you go—the faster you spend—the greater the potential for a big crash. The more sales and commission you make, the more you want and **expect** to make.

Unquestionably the most exciting thing about being a commission salesperson is the unlimited income you can earn, and you are reminded of this every day, from the day you start work to the day you finish. It is exciting, but it can also become exhausting to go through meetings every week and compete with your fellow agents to see who made more sales and money.

Unfortunately, many real estate agents burn out after just a few short years and leave the industry. So, to eliminate many of the myths that surround the real estate industry, this is a good spot to mention a few little-known truths.

In Australia, the average full-time wage is $81,530.80 per year.
On average, Australian workers work 40.3 hours per week.
The average wage for a real estate agent in Australia is $77,417.60 per year.
I suspect real estate agents in Australia work far more than 40 hours per week.
(Source: Australian Bureau of Statistics)

For some added perspective, I have also provided comparable information for realtors in the United States:

The median income for American realtors is $42,500 per year.
The median wage in America is $53,612 per year.
American realtors with 16+ years of experience have a median income of $78,850 per year.
American realtors with two years or less experience have a median income of $8,930 per year.
48% of American realtors have two years or less experience at their present firm.
The average number of hours worked in the United States per week is 34.5 (across all industries).
American realtors work on average 40 hours per week (though I suspect this figure is extremely conservative, based on the amount of after-hours and weekend work involved in being a successful agent).
(Source: National Association of Realtors 2017 Member Profile and U.S. Bureau of Labor Statistics 2018.)

I am not mentioning these statistics to be controversial or to denigrate an industry that I love, but simply to make you aware of a few facts that very few people think of. More importantly, I want to make the point that *not every agent can be a superstar*.

That doesn't mean you shouldn't try. With enough dedication and adherence to correct procedures, you **can** be a superstar. That's the exciting thing about real estate: regardless of your age, colour, sex, or education level, you can be a superstar. All the training, seminars, and workshops you attend are designed to turn you into one. Unfortunately, though, not every agent is going to make it, and many will just have to accept they are average.

Another important fact about stars is that whether they are in our galaxy or sitting at a desk next to yours, they all eventually fade out.

Consider this, too—there simply aren't enough homes listed for sale for every agent to become a superstar. If overnight, every "average" real estate agent magically became a superstar and tripled the number of sales they were making, where would all the new listings come from? You would run out of homes to sell very quickly.

I am not trying to dampen your drive and enthusiasm. You can still be an exceptional agent and make an excellent salary even if you are not a superstar. There is, however, a way to make a secondary, passive income while you are working in real estate, without doing any extra study or work, and without expending any great effort. In my experience, after many years working as an estate agent and attending countless training seminars and workshops, no one in the real estate industry is talking about this, even though it's a subject we deal with every day.

That subject is **personally investing in rental properties**. No one is better equipped to do this than the agent who lives and breathes real estate every day, but surprisingly few estate agents take advantage of all the knowledge they have accumulated and invest in real estate.

After I had worked as an estate agent for a number of years, I had built up my knowledge of the area in which I worked and had also developed an extensive client base that included investors. Many of these investors came back to me year after year, looking to buy another investment property to add to their portfolio. Some of the investors I worked with could be described as having a very keen interest and even extensive knowledge of real estate investing, but nevertheless, when it came time to buy another property, they would still come to me (and no doubt other real estate agents) to discuss what had been happening in the real estate market.

They wanted to check all the things I mentioned earlier: house-price movements, vacancy rates, rental returns, and so on. These investors would have had their own ideas and opinions, but they still found it prudent to check the facts and get other opinions from local experts. Because I worked in real estate every day and these investors did not, I was a valuable source of information.

After helping these investors for a few years, I began to think about our relationship and what we gained from it. The benefit to me was obvious and immediate: I would make a commission, which meant more money in the next month's pay packet. I didn't consider the benefit to the investor until I looked back, often years later, at the properties they had bought. The properties I sold to the investor now looked to have been cheap. It wasn't because they had been bought below the market price or were particularly cheap or good buys at the time; it was just that the market had kept on moving and growing and changing after the deal was done.

Now the investor had a property that looked like a great buy. They had equity in it and a tenant paying for most, if not all, of the related expenses. Once more, the investor would come back and meet with me to buy another property. And from the transaction I made another month's salary, but the investor was building an income that could potentially continue forever.

I realised I had taken a very short-term view of our transactions, but the investor had taken a much longer-term view that was going to continue paying dividends. Overall, our dealings were far more profitable for the investor than for me. It was then that I finally understood I wasn't thinking enough about my future beyond the next month, and I certainly wasn't taking advantage of everything I had learned. Investors were taking advantage of me.

I am not saying you should stop providing outstanding service to your investors. You should not withhold information or treat them any differently from how you have been. There are plenty of investment properties for everyone, including you and your clients. All I am suggesting is that real estate agents who are not already investing in real estate should start being a little selfish and think about themselves and their future.

In the following chapters, I explain exactly why all estate agents should buy investment properties and why real estate agencies should encourage them to do so.

1

THE NICK

The most important rule when you buy any investment is that you must get it for the right price. Pay too much and it can be an anchor around your neck; you could drown in debt.

When an estate agent is asked to appraise a property for sale, they try to guess what price the owner wants, what competing agents will say, and how buyers will react to the property. These factors account for small variations in appraisal figures between different agents. Larger variations occur when an agent tries to "buy" the listing by promising the owner a hugely inflated sale price, or if an agent doesn't like the property or the prospect of working with the owner and they lowball the estimated sale price in the hope the property will be given to another estate agent to sell.

If you asked an estate agent, "What is a fair market price for this property?", and the agent would have to buy it with their own hard-earned money to sell it to a buyer, as many retailers do to stock their shops, they would know exactly what the property was worth. They would not have to guess, and they would not tailor their estimate to what they thought other agents might say to win the business. My point is that all estate agents, perhaps with the exception of those who have worked in the industry for less than six months, can accurately appraise the value of a property in their area within a few percent of what it's truly worth.

The reason I have qualified this statement by excluding agents with less than six months' experience is that this is about how long it takes for someone new to an area and the industry to become fully competent at appraising a property's value. When I worked in real estate, I often brought new agents with me to appraise properties. This was not just to teach them how to conduct a market appraisal, but also so they could learn about property values in the area. I found that most agents could accurately gauge the value of a property after six months; by that time, they had been on enough appraisals with an experienced estate agent, attended enough auctions, and seen enough sales results from our own office and those of our competitors to have the comparable sales evidence they needed to draw on in reaching their own valuation.

There are also many fantastic websites that can help estate agents and the public when trying to work out what a property is really worth.

When an estate agent has enough knowledge and experience to confidently and accurately appraise the value of a property, they should be looking for suitable investment properties for themselves as much for their clients. In my first book, *How to Buy Unlimited Investment Properties*, I explain how to carry out due diligence and the importance of doing extensive research before buying a property to ensure you do not pay too much. Estate agents are extremely fortunate that every day at work is part of their due diligence, and the best part is that they are being paid.

The estate agent's advantage as an investor

Estate agents have an advantage over every buyer and seller because their knowledge of their area is unmatched. Sure, most buyers and sellers will be aware of some sale results, and they may believe they are experts, but their knowledge is only a fraction as broad and comprehensive as the agent's. Estate agents should be taking advantage of this knowledge. There is nothing unethical about using what you learn while working as an agent to your advantage, and it is not unfair or detrimental to others if you buy an investment property for yourself. There are enough properties for sale to satisfy everyone.

I am sure that from time to time an estate agent will comb through the internet or local newspaper and come across a property listed for sale at a price that seems too good to be true—well below market value. You often can't believe how lucky the estate agent must have been to list it for sale at that price, because they are assured of making a quick commission. These properties are commonly referred to as "nicks". Sometimes things are exactly as they look: "too good to be true". The property may be listed for sale at a very low price because it is falling apart and needs extensive work just to make it habitable, let alone appealing.

Other times, though, there is nothing structurally wrong with such a property, and it just needs some tender loving care to revive it and make it appeal to buyers. The seller, for a number of reasons, could be extremely motivated to sell their property, and is unwilling to do some work to make it more appealing to buyers, or does not know how. In this case, the nick is a good property, poorly presented.

The ethics of investing as an estate agent

An estate agent should swoop on properties like this. For reasons of ethics and professionalism, I don't suggest you should buy such a property if it is listed for sale with your own real estate agency. If you do buy a property from your own agency, it opens a can of worms regarding conflict of interest. Whose best interest are working for? If you are trying to get the lowest price for yourself, this certainly isn't in the owner's interest, and I believe this is clearly inappropriate. You would also be depriving yourself and your agency from making a greater sales commission.

There is no shortage of real estate for sale, so you certainly don't need to court those problems that would come from buying from your own agency. A nick will present itself somewhere else soon enough. When one does appear, most agents will grumble that their competitor doesn't have to work hard for their money, as someone will snap up the bargain quickly. Then they forget about it.

But the next time you see a nick, *you* could call the real estate agent handling the sale and ask for an inspection. Be upfront and let the agent know that you are not trying to poach their listing: you are genuinely looking to buy an investment property in the area. If you are friendly and honest, the selling estate agent will be accommodating and more than happy to show you through the property. One day, you may return the favour: if the selling agent becomes a buyer, you can show them through properties you have for sale.

Taking advantage of your knowledge and buying investment properties is a natural progression from your day-to-day job. Car mechanics service their own cars, builders build their own homes, and stockbrokers buy shares for themselves. You would not expect these people to employ someone else to do the job that they can do. Of course a builder will build his or her own house and not use another building company. They do this to take advantage of their knowledge, to save money, and because, as the adage goes, "if you want something done properly, [you] do it yourself." The same goes for the mechanic and stockbroker.

Some readers might think that estate agents buying investment properties seems a bit like insider trading and that you would be taking advantage of unsuspecting people. This is entirely false. Only if you buy a property from your own real estate agency could you be accused of taking advantage of an owner. If you buy a nick from another agency, that is simply good business. Remember, if you don't buy the property, someone else will. As the buyer, you didn't tell the owner what price to put on the property, you didn't give them any advice, and you didn't make any recommendations. This is an arms-length transaction between a willing seller and a willing buyer; it's just that you, the buyer, happen to be an estate agent.

It is perfectly understandable that estate agents are focused on making the next sale and commission, rather than looking for long-term investment opportunities, because the importance of sales and commissions is constantly being reinforced at each sales meeting. But there is nothing stopping estate agents looking for other opportunities to make money that won't interfere with their primary goal of making commission.

If you buy a property at a genuinely discounted price, below market value, you have immediately made money. If, for instance, you buy a property for $450,000 and then have it valued by an independent valuer at $500,000, you have made $50,000. This is your money, and you can use it any way you like. You can buy more investment properties, or you can buy groceries; the choice is entirely yours. But the point is that you have made an extra $50,000 on top of your salary by taking advantage of information that you already have as an estate agent. You would have freely given that information away to any person that asked you about real estate, and you still can. Your investment hasn't interfered with your job, and it hasn't stopped you making commissions. I am sure that anyone would answer yes if asked whether they'd like to make an extra $50,000 on top of their salary without doing too much extra work to get it.

When you have bought a "nick" and made money through the equity you have created in the property, there are ways you can release this money, and that's when investing in real estate becomes really exciting. You can "flip" the property (resell it at a higher price), or you can refinance it.

If you decide to **resell** the property, you may again be able to take advantage of your real estate knowledge and improve the value of the property by carrying out cosmetic improvements to make it more appealing to buyers. Often, improvements can be as easy as painting, recarpeting, or cleaning up the garden. If you are unsure what improvements would best maximise the property's appeal and resale price, get some advice from your real estate colleagues. With enough advice from experienced agents, you should be able to ensure you do not overlook any improvement that could increase your bottom line.

If you want more information on what improvements you should and shouldn't undertake, you can refer to my second book, *Buy Unlimited Investment Properties and Retire in 10 Years*.

If you choose to **refinance,** you can draw upon your newfound equity. You can decide to withdraw the money and spend it on anything you wish, or you could use the equity to buy another investment property and expand your portfolio.

Buying an investment property and making money will not distract you from your main job, which is listing and selling real estate. You look on the internet and through local newspapers every week as part of your job, to keep abreast of what is happening in your real estate market. You need to know what properties are listed for sale and what your competitors are doing. Next time you look, keep in the back of your mind that you might just be the buyer for the next "nick". It actually makes looking through the newspapers and internet a lot more exciting.

2

MANAGING YOUR INVESTMENT

So far, it may appear that sales consultants are best placed to take advantage of the knowledge they gain at work in a real estate agency. But actually, behind every good investment property there is a very good property manager. Just like sales consultants, property managers can take advantage of their knowledge when they become investors.

While a sales consultant is well-equipped to identify a "nick", a property manager can identify a great rental property: they know what tenants are looking for. They also know the profile of tenants looking in the area: whether the area mostly attracts families, single people, or professional couples. They know whether tenants prefer bigger living spaces or bigger bedrooms, and big back gardens or smaller courtyards.

A property manager knows what tenants like and want, and what they are prepared to pay for it. Most importantly, a property manager knows how to accurately ascertain what a property can achieve in rent and what improvements can be made to maximise the rental return.

Working out what a property will rent for is an important skill, because often properties will be advertised for sale with an estimated rental figure shown. With their limited knowledge of actual rents in an area, interested buyers will rely upon that estimate. This is particularly true in new large-scale developments, where rental estimates are almost always provided, often accompanied by a rental guarantee from the developer. These rental estimates always lean towards being generous, and the rental guarantee is provided to cover any shortfall.

As an example, imagine a property for sale is being advertised with an estimated rental figure of $550 per week, but in reality, the property can only achieve rent of $475 per week. If the property is being sold with a rental guarantee, the developer will pay the difference between the two figures (in this case $75 per week) for the term of the guarantee (usually one to two years). This sounds wonderful for the buyer, as they are guaranteed to receive the higher rental figure for the agreed period. The problem comes later when the guarantee runs out and the buyer can only attract market-level rent. In this example, the difference between the rental guarantee and the market rent (which is $75 per week) may not seem a lot of money, but over a whole year it adds up to $3,900.

If the buyer relies on the higher rent to service their loan repayments, they could face a financial problem when the rental guarantee expires. Obviously, any change in your rental income will change the way your investment is geared, and if rent falls significantly, it will negatively affect your cash flow. Assuming a higher rent than is realistic can be a very costly mistake for those who are new to investing in real estate. An experienced property manager is far less likely to fall into this trap, since they can accurately determine what the true market rent is for a property in the area.

Maximising the rental return often takes different improvements to those that would maximise the property's resale price. For instance, painting the outside of a property can make it look prettier and attract a better resale price, but probably won't get you more rent. Likewise, doing some landscaping outside can get you a better price when the time comes to sell, but tenants are unlikely to pay more rent because you added a few more plants and put some woodchips on the garden beds.

Tenants looking for a property to live in have a different perspective from people who want to buy a home. First, tenants expect to live in a property for a shorter term (normally one or two years), where homebuyers will typically expect to live there seven years or more. As a result, tenants don't want a property that needs renovations: they want a home that is comfortable and ready to live in now, not after they've redone the bathrooms and kitchen. A tenant will look at the number of bedrooms in a property, the size of the living space and back garden, and the condition of the wet areas (e.g. bathrooms, toilets, the kitchen and laundry, etc.). These are the main factors that determine the amount of rent payable. Things like the exterior colour of the property will have little to no impact on the rent.

To maximise rental income, property managers will assess what improvements a property might need. These could be little things like adding shelving or cupboards to the garage, or erecting a small garden shed in the backyard, to give the tenant more storage space; installing ceiling fans in the bedroom to make them more comfortable in summer; or installing heaters or air conditioners in individual rooms. Larger improvements might include renovating a bathroom to include a bathtub, to help attract families, or removing the bathtub and installing a double shower to attract professional couples. The smaller improvements particularly help to attract potential tenants and increase the rental return, but they will likely make little difference to the property's resale price—except insofar as increased rental returns boost its value.

The correlation between rental return and sale price

Improving a property to increase the rental return is always a good idea. Apart from increasing the amount of money the investor makes every week, when the time comes to sell the property, most estate agents, valuers, and investors will take note of the rental income received, because there is a correlation between what a property is worth and the rental income it generates.

Let's consider our earlier example again, where a developer sold a property with a rental guarantee of $550 per week but the actual market rent was $475. This property may have looked attractive on the surface, but as a potential buyer, you need to question the developer's motive for providing the guarantee. By advertising the property with a rent of $550 per week, the developer can justify a higher sale price for the property, because of the correlation between rental income and sale price. By getting an extra $10,000 or $20,000 on the sale price, the developer has effectively covered the cost of the guarantee, which was $3,900 per year (the difference between $475 and $550 per week, multiplied by 52 weeks). The rental guarantee was a very cost-effective marketing tool designed purely to justify a higher asking price and attract unwitting investors.

Typically, sales consultants and property managers look at what improvements need to be made to a property from different perspectives. It is preferable to consider any improvements from both points of view.

The property manager's advantages as an investor

The most obvious advantage that a property manager has, as an investor, is that they can manage their own property. A good property manager needs great communication skills, extensive knowledge of legislation, incredible organisation, superb time-management skills, and the calmness and patience of a saint. Most investors do not possess all these skills, so they should use a property manager to look after their investment property, and naturally they must pay management fees to the real estate agency when they do so. A property manager should be able to save on some, if not all, of these costs by managing the property themselves.

But the advantages extend beyond saving a few dollars. The property manager's biggest and best advantage is that they can choose who rents their property, and they will ensure that the tenant is looking after it and the investment is being well managed.

Most experienced property managers have encountered a situation where an investment property has, for no apparent reason or fault, struggled to attract good rental applications. Fortunately, these instances are rare, but that makes them no less frustrating for the owner and the property manager.

Sometimes a property is just unlucky, but at other times, it might struggle to attract a tenant because the owner has been stubborn about asking for an extra $10 a week in rent. Regardless of the reasons, whenever a property is vacant for long, the investor usually becomes impatient and starts making more demands of the property manager. If they do not find a tenant soon, the investor will invite other real estate agencies to look for one. There becomes a much greater likelihood that the property manager will lose the listing, which can diminish their pay. Understandably, this puts pressure on the property manager, who will start to consider even those rental applications where the prospective tenants do not have great references.

When a property manager looks after the management of their own rental property, they can take steps to ensure that they do not become the victim of a long rental vacancy, and they can also make sure their property is only rented to excellent tenants. I am not suggesting property managers take less care of their clients' investment properties if they are vacant for a longer period, but to keep anxious clients happy and avoid losing the rental management, they may lower the bar when it comes to selecting a suitable tenant. The final decision as to who rents the property always rests with the owner, but recommendations from the property manager can have a big influence when the time comes to make the final decision.

Property managers know the importance of having a great tenant living in a rental property. Unfortunately, the reputation of tenants in general is unjustifiably tarnished by the actions of a small minority that damage properties or are poor payers, continuously behind on their rent. Some tenants take exceptional care of the property they live in, often much better than many owner-occupiers. They attend to the garden and keep an exceptionally clean home. They are undemanding, and courteous to the owner and property manager.

These tenants are not as hard to find as you may think, and they enjoy a special place in the heart of every property manager. When they are looking to move into another rental property, the property manager will do everything in their power to make sure they find a suitable property for these tenants so they continue to rent through their agency. If a property manager is looking after the management of their own investment property and such a tenant comes along, they understand that the benefits of having a great tenant outweigh the extra $10 per week in rent they might get from another, perhaps less desirable tenant. So, when these great tenants look for a rental property, a property manager should and will prioritise showing them through their own investment property.

In my experience, another advantage that property managers have is something all real estate offices experience, but which is largely not spoken of and certainly not written in any policy. This is that tradespeople often discount work they do on a home or investment property owned by a property manager who regularly passes them work.

Property managers keep a list of preferred tradespeople who are fully qualified, insured, and reliable, and can be called upon quickly to carry out maintenance and repairs. Tradespeople covet their positions on such preferred lists. When they are on such a list, they will get regular work from the property manager, for which they will be paid on time. As a result, such tradespeople will do high-quality work at very competitive rates, typically much lower than investors would be offered privately. Often, these competitive rates are further reduced or even (for small jobs) totally ignored when tradespeople work on the property manager's own properties. Since it is so valuable for the tradesperson to stay on the preferred list, it is worth them doing the occasional small job for free for the property manager to help foster a good relationship—it is an investment for the future. This aside, it is relatively easy for a property manager to get the best price possible for maintenance and repairs on their investment properties, and to make sure that the work is done to the highest standard.

The property manager's duties

There are many important duties that all property managers perform for their clients, and two of the most crucial are making a detailed ingoing condition report before a new tenant moves in, and performing a routine inspection every six months after that (or when legislation permits).

Arguably, the ingoing condition report is the second-most-important document in the property file, after the lease agreement. It records the condition the property is in before a new tenant moves in. These reports are used when tenants vacate a property, to compare the condition when they leave to when they moved in. From these reports, the property manager can determine if the tenant has kept the property in good condition or if damage has occurred. If there has been any damage, a claim can be lodged against the bond (paid as a deposit by the tenant when they begin their tenancy) to pay for repairs or compensate the property owner.

These condition reports are incredibly important, and the property manager must complete them thoroughly and accurately. In my experience, every rental property managed by a property manager has a condition report, but how comprehensive these reports are depends on how good the property manager is and how much care they have taken.

If a claim is made against the bond, the condition report is the star witness, and the property manager will be judged by how good the report is in supporting the case. If a condition report has not been completed correctly, accurately, or comprehensively, the property owner's chance of receiving compensation for damage caused by the tenant is greatly diminished. Any property manager looking after their own rental property will make sure that the condition report is as thorough and detailed as it can possibly be.

Routine inspections are carried out to ensure that the tenant is keeping the property in good condition and complying with the rental agreement. Legislation permits the owner or property manager to perform regular inspections during the term of the lease, and while these inspections are very important, it is my experience that when some property managers become inundated with work, these inspections can be overlooked.

Sometimes, after a routine inspection has been carried out, the property manager may tell the tenant to rectify something. Typically, this will be a small matter, like cleaning up part of the property or removing built-up rubbish, but it could be something more significant like removing a pet from the property when no permission has been given to keep it there. When there are matters like this to be resolved, the property manager's duty is to follow up with the tenant and arrange another inspection to ensure the required action has been taken. Again, when they are overwhelmed with other jobs, property managers may not get around to checking that the tenant has adhered to the instructions. Any property manager looking after their own rental property will make sure that all routine inspections are carried out, that tenants are looking after their property, and that they are abiding by the terms of the lease.

3

ATTRACT MORE CLIENTS

Real estate is a numbers game. It's all about the number of phone calls you make, appraisals you conduct, clients and listings you have, sales you make, properties you rent, etc. The higher the numbers, the more successful you are, and the more money you will make for yourself and the agency.

Every task in real estate has a number attached to it. Every number can be measured, scrutinised, compared, and dissected. There isn't a single task in the industry that can't be quantified in some way, but in the end, the most important number—the one that makes you money—is the number of clients you have.

Attract more clients by becoming an investor

To attract more clients, buy investment properties. If you build a property portfolio for yourself, you will attract more clients, particularly investors, for two very similar reasons:

- They have made a *conscious* decision to only work

with and take advice from someone who has achieved what they want to achieve.
- They are attracted to you *subconsciously* because they would like to deal with someone who is successful. Dealing with a successful estate agent gives them confidence that you can help them achieve what they want to.

In the preface, I mentioned the importance of dealing with someone who has achieved what you want to achieve. This takes conscious effort. There are many naysayers in this world who will quickly and efficiently extinguish your dreams, and they are motivated to do so because if you succeed in reaching your goals, you will expose their failings and insecurities.

Do not listen to these people. It is often easier said than done, because such naysayers are all around and may be people very close to us. If you listen to all the cynics, a seed of doubt will grow in you until you cannot act because you are paralysed by the fears others have planted. Remember that the biggest critics are often the people who have been too timid and scared to give something a try.

When you are a successful estate agent and property investor, you will attract more clients because there are buyers and sellers out there who have consciously decided, just as I recommend, that they will not listen to naysayers and only take advice from people who are achieving what they want to achieve. Most of these new clients will be investors who understand that taking advice from an estate agent who is actively investing in the same area they are interested in is far better than listening to someone who can tell them a bunch of theories but has never practised what they preach.

The second group of clients you will attract are those who are drawn to you on a subconscious level. In fact, you have been trying to attract these clients from the moment you started your career in real estate. That's why you dress smartly, wear an expensive suit, clean your shoes, buy an expensive car, and have the latest smartphone. You are trying to give the impression that you are already successful, because people want to deal with successful people, particularly when it involves something as important as real estate—which in most cases is a person's most valuable asset.

Prove your success

Only in exceptional cases, such as if they had a relative starting a new career in real estate, would someone selling or renting a property consider giving their listing (and entrusting their valuable asset) to an inexperienced estate agent who is unproven and will potentially be unsuccessful. A client wants to feel confident that no matter what happens along the way, whatever challenges and unforeseen problems may pop up, their estate agent can handle it. If you are personally investing in real estate to build your portfolio and wealth, your clients will feel confident in your abilities. Most of the new clients you attract this way will be property owners looking for a successful agent to sell their property or manage their investment property.

You don't need to shout your success from the roof of the tallest building. In fact, this would prove disastrous, because people love nothing more than tearing down a tall poppy. If you are successful and have an ego the size of Texas, you will repel more clients than you attract. It is true that clients and people in general wish to deal with successful people, but they also tend to want those people to be humble.

Letting people know you own investment properties in the local area is not something you should brag about—and you don't need to. It's enough that when you are asked for an opinion about real estate, particularly something that concerns your local market, you can simply add something like, "That's why I bought in this area." The rest will take care of itself. If people know you have investment properties, they will ask you about them and all you need to do is answer honestly and openly. In my experience, people love talking about real estate. It doesn't matter if they own real estate themselves, or whether they are a doctor, lawyer, carpenter, or follow any other profession. Regardless of their background, many people are fascinated by real estate. If you are an estate agent and you personally own investment properties, in the eyes of the public your credentials have just grown enormously.

There is no limit to the number of new clients you can attract this way. It may start slowly. Initially, you may only attract a few friends who want to invest in real estate just like you. Then an investor may become your client, and they will refer other investors to you for advice and to expand their own portfolios. Gradually, the landlords who have rental properties managed through your agency will learn that you are actively investing in the area and will contact you before buying any more properties in the area. The number of good, qualified buyers you have looking to buy an investment property from you in the next year or two will steadily grow, and most of that will occur organically through referrals, requiring very little effort on your part. And experienced real estate agents know that the best client is always one that has been referred to you.

All estate agents also know buyers will one day become sellers. Investors who bought an investment property with your help will one day need your help to sell, and who better to list their property with than you? Just as your number of buyers builds up, so does the number of vendors you have.

Be the local expert

Your goal is to be known as the **local expert**. Of course, you won't sell or manage every investment property in the area, but you would like your clients to deal exclusively with you and consider you their go-to expert. When a new property is listed for sale by your real estate agency, you want to have a list of qualified investors who are ready to buy right away, based on your recommendations.

These investors know you, and you know them. You have built up rapport and trust. You can explain all the features of the property that make it an attractive investment and why *you* would buy it if you could. Your regular buyers have trust and faith in you and the properties you recommend. Of course, they aren't going to buy every property you recommend, but if you have a list of qualified investors you have been working with, you should be confident that one of them will jump at the opportunity. The list doesn't have to be massive, but it must be made of investors who are actively looking and would like to buy another investment property within the next one to two years. If an investor hasn't bought an investment property in, say, the past five years, you need to question how motivated they are to expand their portfolio.

From time to time, one of "your" investors will seek your advice on a new investment property they have found through another agency. It is important that you are honest with your opinions and advice. If the property is good, tell your client that. You will build up far more trust and loyalty with that client if you are honest. Likewise, if you find a "nick" (a concept we covered in chapter 1) and you aren't in a position to buy it yourself, tell your clients. If you have a list of clients looking to buy an investment property and you refer them to another estate agent's listing, what is the worst-case scenario? You may lose one client off your list for now, but the loyalty and trust you build with them and anyone they know is immeasurable. Your clients will see that you really are looking after their best interests and will make them aware of all the best available investment properties regardless of who has listed them. If you do this for your clients, they will eventually stop looking in the papers and on the internet for investment properties themselves, because they trust that you are doing the work for them. This also means that your clients are not speaking with other estate agents, and therefore you are far more likely to retain your clients over a long period.

I am not suggesting that you make a monthly habit of referring your clients to other real estate agencies' listings. I would only do this once or twice a year, and only when you have truly found a nick. But doing it once or twice a year makes a lasting impression on your clients. If you do refer one of your clients to another agency to buy an investment property, you could also ask for a referral fee from that agency. Depending on your relationship with that agency, you may get a share of the sale commission, but the long-term benefit you receive is far more valuable than a once-off commission. You are in the business of building clients for life. I would, however, insist that the investor I referred to the property gives it to our real estate agency to manage. My main reason for doing this is not to make a few dollars for the rental department, but to keep my relationship with the client. If their investment property is managed through a competing real estate agency, that agency has the chance to build rapport and a relationship with my client. I don't want to give my competitors that opportunity.

Remember, sharing information honestly and in your clients' interest is about making more clients for life who will always ask you first before they do anything concerning real estate.

4

INVESTMENT SEMINARS

Another great way to attract more clients and become known as the expert in your local area is to run investment seminars. Many real estate agencies have held investment seminars, with varying degrees of success. Regardless of the number of people who attend, these seminars are a fantastic opportunity to build your client database and awareness of your brand. The problem is usually that real estate agencies hold an investment seminar once and then never hold another one, or that years pass between these seminars. As with all prospecting activities, you get rewarded for consistency of effort. Doing something once may bring you limited success, but doing the same thing over and over compounds the rewards over time.

If you run investment seminars, you will naturally attract people who are interested in real estate, particularly if it is free to attend. People love to get something for nothing. The people attending the seminar will most likely be an eclectic group with a range of reasons for attending. The audience will most likely include buyers interested in investing in real estate (both novice and experienced investors), first-homebuyers trying to break into the market, mum-and-dad investors thinking about starting up a self-managed superannuation fund, homeowners thinking of selling who want to know how to maximise their sale price, and many others.

An investment seminar is a great opportunity to meet all these people and develop databases that you can nurture over time. You can stay in regular contact with them through phone calls, letters, pamphlets, and newsletters. Many of these people will come along to your investment seminar even though they have dealt with another real estate agency and may never have had dealings with yours. The seminar is, therefore, a fantastic opportunity to poach some of your competitors' clients.

The features and benefits of a good investment seminar

The important features of any good investment seminar are that it must include a call to action and be specific to your area.

There could be one call to action or several. Examples include:

- As a thank you to those attending the seminar, if they speak with one of your staff at the end and transfer the management of their investment property to your firm, you will give them a discounted management fee for a year or free management fees for the first two months.
- The chance to buy a particular investment property in a new development before it sells out.
- List a property for sale with your firm within the next 48 hours to receive a discounted commission rate or cheaper marketing fees.

The possibilities are endless, but the aim is to have a measurable result at the end of the seminar. How many people have you added to your database? How many new rental properties for management did you attract? How many new listings or sales did you gain?

Some of the benefits of running investment seminars are difficult to measure, such as increasing brand awareness, so it is important to have some tangible results at the end that will motivate you to hold more seminars in the future.

One failing of many investment seminars is that they are too broad in their content. They provide too much general information about the real estate market as a whole, and not enough detailed information about a specific area or properties. It is fair to say that most, if not all, of the people attending the seminar have an interest in real estate. Likewise, most, if not all, already have an idea of how the real estate market is going generally. They have listened to news bulletins on television or read in the papers whether real estate prices are rising or falling, and heard what the expectations are for the foreseeable future. They know what the reserve bank and other financial institutions are doing with interest rates. And they have a good idea if rents are going up or down, generally.

But most of these people lack detailed information about the suburb or neighbourhood you specialise in. To make the seminar relevant, you need to talk about what is happening here and now in your area, and because you are the local expert, you are the most qualified person to speak about it. Are rental prices increasing, and if so, by how much? You can give examples of rents paid last year in the area, compared with this year. Likewise, have property values increased? Give examples of properties you have sold this year, and show what they previously sold for. Investors will identify with this information, because it's local, and find it far more informative and interesting than a bulletin on the six-o'clock national news.

All investment seminars should start with broad brushstrokes, outlining what is happening in the real estate market generally. You can cover such things as price movements in capital cities, population growth, interest-rate movements, large-scale infrastructure projects, and so on. Most people will be aware of these facts, but hearing it from you will reinforce what they already believe is true, and demonstrate your credibility by showing you know what is going on

Once you have covered the general market, you need to start focusing on your local market and why people should buy investment properties in your area.

Again, you can start with broad brushstrokes, talking about trends in the local market and gradually drilling down until you are giving very detailed information using examples of specific properties that sold a few years ago and have now resold for a higher or lower price. You can also show specific examples of what has happened to rental prices in the same period. If you can provide real examples of properties in your area, the information becomes more relevant and interesting for your audience, and again, it shows you really know your local market and establishes you as the expert in the area.

Planning your investment seminar

Naturally, when you are planning a seminar, you need to consider what information people want and need. At the same time, though, you also want to let people know exactly why they should buy an investment property from *you* and why *your agency* is the best one to manage their investment.

The reasons for investing in your area will be specific to it, so it is impossible to outline one investment seminar here that would fit everyone. The area you work in may offer better rental yields than the state average, higher median rents, lower vacancy rates, higher capital growth figures over a defined period, higher or lower median house prices, and so on.

Whatever is true, you must tailor the investment seminar to show *why investors should buy in your area*. To add weight to your case, you can include comments such as, "This is why I personally invest in the area."

Here are a few ways you can tailor your seminar to your specific area:

- If you work in an area with a high rental yield, highlight that the gap between what you receive in rent and the interest you pay on an investment loan is reduced. This improves investors' cash flow and gearing, making it easier to afford the property.
- If you work in an area with a low rental yield, it is likely because property prices have increased faster than rents, and you could highlight that your area has experienced higher capital growth. This will appeal to investors who want to build their wealth.
- If you work in an area with an average rental yield, this is great for investors because there is an excellent balance between good rental returns and future capital growth.

When you are talking to potential investors about buying a property in your area, make sure you tell them about all the wonderful things that make it a desirable place for tenants to live. These may include:

- an inner-city location that attracts professional people and couples
- easy access to public transport
- universities and schools in the area that attract students, who mainly live in rental properties
- proximity to trendy bars and cafes, which attracts young professional couples with high disposable incomes
- location in a safe outer suburb, which appeals to families
- proximity to the beach or parks, which offers families and couples a relaxed lifestyle

To add further interest and colour to your seminar, it is good to show photos of properties in your area as real-life examples of what you are describing. Pictures add power to your presentation. Of course, you will show examples of properties that have achieved higher than expected rents or sale prices. Just make sure that you don't oversell your area and give investors inflated expectations of what they could expect to achieve. If you keep showing examples of properties that are rented for $550 per week but the average rent for the area is only $450, you may build an expectation that you can achieve a higher rental for all properties you manage. You don't want to over-promise, which could lead to disappointing clients and losing their trust. Rather, you want to demonstrate that you have a comprehensive knowledge of how investment properties are performing in your area.

5

INVESTMENT GROUPS

In my opinion, the most exciting service an estate agent can offer their clients is to act as a "buyer's advocate" and buy investment properties on behalf of groups of investors. These groups can and should include yourself, and I would encourage you, whenever possible, to buy an investment with your buying group and take advantage of the discounts you achieve.

If you personally buy an investment property in such an investment group, you will add to your investment portfolio, add credibility to your group, and significantly increase your income. In my first book, *How to Buy Unlimited Investment Properties*, chapter 11 ("The Syndicate") describes in greater detail how I started forming buyer groups and how they work. Most importantly, it gives tips on negotiating discounts for bulk purchases. As a result, I won't go into quite as much detail here. But I will give you the most crucial details that will enable you to start your own investment groups.

Please note that although I refer to these groups as "investment" groups that buy "investment" properties, buyers wanting a property to live in are not excluded from joining. Nevertheless, in my experience such groups are mainly made up of investors.

The idea behind forming an investment group is very simple: you want to buy properties in bulk to get a discount. The concept is commonly applied in other areas: consumers regularly buy in bulk to save money. Instead of paying $2 for a single can of soft drink at the supermarket, you can buy a six-pack for $6 ($1 per can, a 50% discount). Savings like these apply to the most mundane of daily items all the way through to luxury items we only buy occasionally. Not only can you buy rolls of toilet paper in bulk, you can even buy hotel stays this way. We also see this applied to services: if you visit a gym once, you might pay $10, but if you pay for 10 visits at a time, the cost might be $50, reducing the cost to $5 per visit. Most people are familiar and comfortable with this kind of practice, and it applies to real estate, too.

Scenarios for buying properties in bulk

To illustrate how this could very easily apply to your real estate purchases, I have made up a scenario that is much like what you could experience in reality:

A friend has asked you, as an estate agent, to look at a property they are interested in buying. The property is part of a new development being built. The asking prices are fixed.

Your friend is very excited about this property, but they have asked you to get involved to see if you can use your negotiation skills to help them get them a better price.

You have a chat with the owner or selling agent, but they tell you sales have been steadily progressing and there is definitely no room for negotiation on the fixed asking price. Despite your best efforts, you can't get the owner to offer a discount. But just when you think the negotiation is over, you ask what discount they would offer if you bought two properties? After a few minutes, the owner or agent offers you a $5,000 discount on each property if you buy two. Then you ask how much more of a discount they would give you if you bought three properties?

Your friend isn't interested in buying two properties, but if you got the price low enough, you might be interested in buying one yourself. If you could find another buyer or two, you could all equally benefit from a larger discount. And if you could earn a commission for securing those properties on behalf of further buyers, it would be a double win for you.

Before you start thinking this scenario seems implausible, consider this: close friends, relatives, and clients often ask estate agents to look at properties they are interested in buying. We usually do this at no cost. Many of us also know someone who has bought a property and despite their best efforts (and ours) has not been able to get any discount on the sale price. Some readers may also have personally encountered a situation where an owner has offered to give a discount on the sale of two or more properties.

The exact scenario I presented is fictitious, but it's not too far from a real-life scenario I participated in, which had many similar characteristics.

Looking at real life, now, I recently found a development under construction that comprised 26 apartments. Of these, 19 had already sold and 7 were left. The apartments were built by a highly regarded developer with an extensive track record of residential developments in Melbourne.

At the time, I was looking to buy an investment property for myself and other investors. Of the apartments that had sold, 18 had gone for the full asking price, while one was sold for $15,000 less because, as the developer explained, the buyer for that apartment had previously bought five other apartments from the same developer but in different locations, and had paid the full asking price for each. The $15,000 discount was given to the buyer as a thank you. I was also told that this particular buyer had personally spent over $3 million on properties with that developer.

The asking prices for this development, and all other developments by this particular developer, were set at the valuation figure provided by a sworn independent valuer on the basis of comparable sales evidence. A copy of the valuation, with supporting evidence, was given to all interested buyers.

I was also informed before negotiations that it was a policy of this developer to give no discounts to any buyer on the sale of any property and, to further emphasise the point, that no discounts would be considered for this specific project due to the strength of the real estate market at the time and the sales already made. If discounts were given, it would undermine the sales already made, I was told. To add further strength to the developer's position, the development was almost sold out just a few weeks after being marketed for sale, well before any construction was due to start.

Regardless, I was only interested in buying the remaining seven apartments if I could obtain a discount for myself and my clients. I was after a discount of at least 5%. I chose this figure because according to figures from the Australian Bureau of Statistics and BIS Shrapnel, between 1960 and 2010 the median house price in Melbourne has never fallen by more than 5% in a single year, so getting a discount at that level makes it very unlikely the value of the property will ever fall below what I and my clients have paid. The largest recorded fall in Melbourne in that period was 4.7% in 1963. In Sydney, for the same period, the largest fall recorded was 5.2% in 1991, which is the only time a fall of above 5% in any year has been recorded. To see complete lists of yearly percentage changes during this period, please see my first book, *How to Buy Unlimited Investment Properties*. Similar results have also been recorded in other capital cities across Australia.

I have given you my reasoning for the level of discount I looked for in that case, but the size of the discount you are after will also depend on the strength of the market at the time. When I was interested in buying those apartments, the real estate market was very strong. Interest rates were at a record low, and property prices were experiencing unprecedented growth. The development I was interested in completely sold out within weeks of being launched for sale, before a single sod was turned. This was a common scenario across the market. But as we know, markets turn: interest rates can go up, consumer confidence can go down, and sales can slow. When this happens, you will be able to negotiate discounts of more than 5%. For the reasons I have pointed out, I will only buy a property if I can negotiate a discount of *at least* 5%.

The combined value of the seven apartments I was interested in buying was $3,745,000. I started negotiations at $3,370,000, 10% below the valuation. The developer quickly declined this offer and the next offer I made, which was 7% below the valuation. We haggled over the next few days, until eventually I secured the last seven apartments for $3,555,000. This was a saving of $190,000, a little more than the 5% discount I was hoping to achieve as my absolute minimum. I then shared this discount equally between all investors by reducing each investor's purchase price (including mine) by the same percentage figure, because the asking price for each apartment was slightly different. As a result, buyers in our group saved $27,000 on average. This was a fantastic outcome for a few reasons:

- If I had tried to buy one apartment, I would not have gotten any discount.
- In total, we spent $3,555,000 and received a discount of $190,000, which was far better than an individual buyer spending over $3,000,000 of their hard-earned money and receiving a $15,000 discount.
- Although collectively we spent $3,555,000, each buyer only spent around $510,000, on average, which is far more affordable.

Results like this can only be achieved when working together in a buying group that flexes its collective negotiating power.

After I agreed to the sale price with the developer, each investor in the group signed a sale contract to buy an apartment in their own name. I have always worked on this basis. Each investor buys their own investment property and builds their own portfolio. I do not jointly own properties with any person other than my wife.

On the same day we settled these property sales with the developer, one of the investors in our group relisted their apartment for sale with a local estate agent. They sold the apartment a short time later for $550,000, which was $37,000 more than they paid, and above the independent valuation figure of $540,000.

I have included a list ("Appendix: Apartment Sales to the Buying Group") at the back of this book that shows the sworn valuation figure for all apartments in that development and the sale prices paid, with the seven apartments we bought highlighted.

The benefits of buying in an investment group

I have achieved similar results to these whenever I have bought properties in bulk in an investment group. The benefits are numerous, for yourself and your clients. This win-win situation is extremely appealing for everyone involved, including your real estate agency, which is precisely why I said, at the start of this chapter, that in my opinion this is the most exciting service you can offer your clients. As an estate agent, your benefits are twofold:

- If you buy an investment property, you also benefit from the discount you have negotiated and save money yourself.
- Because you are forming these investment groups and securing a property for each person in the group, you can charge each person a commission. When you buy multiple properties using this method, you earn multiple commissions. If you buy seven apartments for seven investors, you earn seven commissions, even though you have only been through one negotiation with the seller. It is an extremely efficient and profitable use of your time.

I mentioned earlier that whenever it is possible, I think you should buy a property with the other buyers in your investment group. One reason for this is that it adds credibility to your group. Whenever I have formed a group, I have personally bought a property, because I want to demonstrate to the other buyers that I believe the properties I am putting forward for their consideration are good enough for me to buy personally. If the property is good enough for me, hopefully it will be good enough for my clients. Naturally, if I don't like a property, I won't bring it to the attention of the group.

The benefits of buying properties in an investment group extend beyond just achieving a discounted price. After I have secured the properties, I work on behalf of everyone in the group to find cheaper conveyancing rates (solicitors' fees), bank loans, rental-management fees, and so on. I do all this on behalf of the group so we can share equally in the savings. For instance, when I am discussing conveyancing fees with solicitors, I mention that there are other investors in our group who would like to use their services, and that I want their lowest price based on multiple clients. I secure discounted prices each step of the way. This service is part of the commission I charge my clients, but remember, I am also doing this for my own benefit—I also enjoy the discounted fees from the solicitors and other providers. If, for any reason, a buyer in our group doesn't want to use a conveyancing firm, bank, or real estate managing agent I have negotiated discount fees with, they can use a different firm of their choice. In my experience, this very seldom happens, because buyers are just as keen as I am to get the lowest prices possible. However, on the rare occasions this happens, you can still achieve bulk discounts for the remaining buyers in your group.

When I form an investment group, I discuss the type of properties I am looking for, the services I provide, and, of course, the benefits to clients who join. To be completely transparent, I make clients aware that I am also part of the investment group and that I will also enjoy any benefit I derive for them. They will understand from this that I am determined to get the best result possible for them, and for myself. I keep my clients informed of every step throughout the entire process, from looking for suitable properties to making an offer, and all the way through to negotiating a lower fee with solicitors. I also explain why I charge clients a commission when I already receive a benefit from being a part of our investment group.

Although we all benefit equally from being part of the group, it still takes one person to drive the process and buy the properties. In this case, that's me. If my clients would like to go and form their own groups and do all the work, they may do so, but it takes time, knowledge, and skill. To compensate me for my time, effort, and skill, I need to be paid. After all, while I am spending time searching the market for a fantastic property for them to buy, they are still at their job earning money, and I need to earn money in the same way.

However, the entire premise of forming an investment group is to save money by doing things in bulk, and as I am earning commissions in bulk, I can and do offer my clients a better commission rate than they would get if they employed a real estate buyer's advocate to act on their behalf. If a buyer's advocate normally charges 3% commission for finding a property, I charge 2%, because I am getting this from multiple clients at once. If I have seven clients in the investment group and each person pays me 2% commission, I am effectively making a 14% commission on the average price of one property in the deal.

I also emphasise to clients that the savings I make for them are far more than what they pay me in commission. We saw this clearly in the case of the buyer I mentioned earlier, who sold their property shortly after buying it, for $37,000 more than they paid. This was sufficient to cover all the costs of buying and selling the property, with a small profit left over. If they had paid the full asking price when they bought the property, they would not have been able to sell it right away without losing a considerable amount of money. My commission was only a fraction of the $37,000 increase they achieved in the sale price.

Buying at below market value

If you are to sell a property shortly after buying it, you must buy it for less than its intrinsic market value. Any profit you make will be due to having saved money when you bought it. Because little time has elapsed, it is unlikely that the real estate market will have had enough time for significant capital growth. When you sell, the market will determine the sale price, so you must take your time when negotiating the purchase of a property and ensure you don't pay too much.

I have mentioned that I will only buy an investment property if I can get a discount to at least 5% below the true market value. It is important to make the distinction between a property's asking (sale) price and its market value. We know that the asking price of a property listed for sale is always slightly inflated above the property's true market value to give the owner a negotiating buffer. That buffer may be 5% or more. It is therefore imperative that you work out what the real market value of the property is and negotiate your discount below that figure. If you negotiate the discount off the asking price, you may still be paying above market value.

All negotiations reach a point where, regardless of how many more properties you offer to buy, you simply cannot achieve a higher discount. It may take three buyers to reach this point, or it may take ten, but there will always be that point where the seller simply cannot and will not increase the discount. When you have reached this point, do not add more buyers to the group to buy additional properties, as this will use up your list of investors. Use the minimum number of buyers required to receive the maximum discount. Save any others who might have liked to participate for your next bulk buy. The time will come when you need those extra investors to get a deal over the line.

Signing the sale contracts

After you have secured the properties, the buyers need to sign sale contracts to buy them in their own names. To fairly allocate the properties among the buyers, I give the first choice of property to the first investor who joined. After they have chosen, the second investor chooses, the third, and so on. First come, first served. If an investor decides they don't want to buy a property on that occasion, they can pass and wait until the next time I buy in bulk. I have always given my clients first choice of the properties and waited until last to make my own selection. I do this to make sure my clients are entirely satisfied with their property, and to show that all the properties are equally good and I am not giving myself preferential treatment.

Anyone can form investment groups and buy properties in bulk. The first time I formed such a group, I was not working in real estate. I have since done it on many occasions, mostly as an estate agent. As an estate agent, you are perfectly positioned to form groups like this, because you come into daily contact with people who want to buy a property, and every buyer wants to save money. In my experience, the best buyers for these groups are investors who already own an investment property and want to expand their portfolio. You have access to an abundant supply of these people. If you work in a real estate agency, they are your existing **landlords**. The best way to reach these and other investors is to run investment seminars. That's yet another great reason to run seminars, which I discussed in chapter 4.

One last benefit of forming buyer groups is that stock levels will never again be a problem. Think of your own real estate agency, and the amount of time, effort, energy, and training that goes into every single property you have found to list for sale. Real estate agencies spend an incredible amount of time and resources in trying to build up the number of properties they have for sale. This is understandable, because without having properties listed, you cannot make sales and commissions. But when you are looking for properties on behalf of buying groups, every property listed and every new development, regardless of which real estate agency is handling the sale, is potentially your next commission. There is no shortage of properties for sale, and it is unlikely there ever will be. If you put just a fraction of the energy you spend trying to list a property for sale into forming buyer groups, you will earn commissions faster and in greater numbers than ever before.

6

BECOME A BETTER AGENT

The real estate industry is excellent at training its staff. In my experience, very few industries are as good as real estate when it comes to the sheer number of training courses available. Naturally, each one is designed to make you a better agent, in the hope that you will become a more productive and profitable member of the business. The courses available cover every conceivable aspect of real estate: not only the technical aspects, like when you can serve a tenant with a notice to vacate, but nuances like how to build rapport with your clients. These courses equip real estate agents with all the tools and skills they need to be a success.

Only investing can teach you empathy

So, if this is the case, what can buying properties yourself teach you that a course could not? The answer is empathy.

As an estate agent, you know what needs to happen to make a sale or lease a property. You know the correct order in which documents need to be signed and who must get a copy. You know how to complete your files and ensure the correct commission is charged. And you *think* you know what the buyer and seller are going through, and how the tenant and landlord feel—but unless you have personally experienced it, you actually don't.

Real estate agents who have bought their own home or investment property, or who have sold their own property, understand this. Most, if not all, agents have been involved in an auction or negotiation where the buyer's offer is not quite at the level acceptable to the vendor, or the level we expected. When this occurs, we usually become frustrated at the seemingly silly, stubborn attitude and behaviour of the short-sighted buyer. If they would just raise their hand at the auction one more time, or increase their offer by only a small amount, we would all be happy. The buyer would win the day and buy the property, the vendor would be excited they have sold it, and you could go home happy that you have made another sale. But the truth is, our greatest motivation for getting the buyer to pay more is not their happiness or that of the seller: we just want to make a commission for all our hard work. I have been guilty of thinking this way, and I am sure all agents have had these exact same thoughts at some stage.

In our race to make another sale, we can easily forget, or simply not understand, the emotional turmoil our clients are experiencing. Not until you have bid at an auction, or been involved in a lengthy negotiation to buy or sell a property for yourself, will you truly appreciate and understand the wave of conflicting emotions you feel. As a buyer, your head is reminding you of all the due diligence you have carried out to determine what a fair market price would be, but your heart is telling you about all the wonderful days and nights you imagine spending with your partner, family, and friends in the home. If you are an estate agent who has never bought their own property, you understand what the buyer is going through in theory only, not from experience.

A very important part of our learning process as real estate agents is to truly understand and appreciate what our clients are going through, so that we can help them more effectively. That is why buying investment properties yourself will make you a better agent.

Anyone selling their home or investment property experiences the same emotional turmoil. The dream price they want to achieve battles in their mind with the basement price they won't go below. Their head and their heart are often in conflict. Hopefully, in the end they will sell their property and be happy with the outcome, but even then, a little voice in the back of their head will always wonder if they should have added another $5,000 to their reserve price before the auction, or countered the buyer's last offer just one more time. Such thoughts and emotions are present every time someone sells a property, and they are perfectly natural. When you sell your own property, you will experience these feelings, and then you will truly understand what your clients are going through.

Learning from your experiences as a client

Empathy is one reason for buying your own properties, and further learning is another. When you become a buyer or seller yourself, you become the client, and you will deal with estate agents from a different perspective to what you normally experience at work. As a buyer or seller, you will be on other real estate agents' databases. You will be the client, and you will know what it feels like to receive phone calls from agents seeking feedback on properties you have inspected or appraisals that have been carried out on your property.

This is very educational. Did you receive follow-up calls? Did you receive too many, or not enough? Was the agent helpful and informative? Were they dismissive and in a rush to get rid of you, or were they generous with their time? Did they seem knowledgeable, or evasive?

When you experience something the estate agent did that you really liked or disliked, you will make sure that incorporate it or remove it from your own behaviour and presentation. For instance, if you liked the way the agent answered a question about marketing costs, you will make a mental note of it in case you can answer the same way one day. Conversely, if it annoyed you that the agent ran late for an appointment with you, in future you will try harder to be on time for appointments with your clients.

You don't want to become a carbon copy of another agent, but we can't help but take small components of people we have met and mesh them into the person we become. As an auctioneer, I experience this regularly. Whenever I see another auctioneer in action, I can't help but evaluate their performance, and I always find things they say or do that I like or dislike. If I don't like something I hear, I will make a mental note to never say those things myself, but if I like certain things, I will file those words away mentally to use later. When you train to become an auctioneer, this is how you learn. You practice on your colleagues, with lots of role-playing. You take bits and pieces from lots of different auctioneers and make them your own. We are, after all, a product of our environment.

The main point of buying investment properties is unquestionably to make money and create wealth for ourselves. One of the welcome side-benefits of buying and selling real estate, regardless of whether it is a home to live in or an investment property, is that you will become a better real estate agent. Buying and selling real estate has a huge learning curve, and it cannot be taught in a classroom.

If you become a better agent, you will naturally make more money. I cannot quantify how much better you will become after you have bought and sold real estate for yourself, and I cannot tell you how much more money you will make. But I *can* assure you that you will have more empathy for your clients, which will lead you to build greater rapport with them. This will lead to happier clients and more referrals. You will become a better real estate agent, and as a result you will make more money.

7

MAKE MORE MONEY

It is not unreasonable or greedy to want to make more money. Most of us work hard for it. It is, after all, the main reason most people get up in the morning and head off to jobs they do not particularly love. If we didn't get paid for going to work, few people would show up. We go to work to make money, and we want more of it to make our lives easier (or at least seemingly easier) and more fun.

A typical career path in real estate goes like this: you begin in the sales, rental, or administration department, and stay there for a few years with little or no advancement. As a sales consultant or property manager, you can make more money through commissions and bonuses, but there are no year-to-year pay increases for longevity or experience. Any pay rises come courtesy of your individual efforts. If a sales consultant or property manager can show they are a proven performer, they may be rewarded by having the word "senior" added to their title, so they become a senior sales consultant or senior property manager. I was never sure if that meant you were considered good, or just getting old!

After that, if your real estate agency is big enough, you

may be able to work up to the role of sales manager, or manager of the rental department. At that point, you have usually hit your head on the corporate ceiling and your career path ends. The most ambitious (not necessarily the most talented) real estate agents will then go on to complete further studies so they can open their own real estate office.

This is the career path I followed. There is certainly nothing wrong with it, and many before and after me will follow the same path. As I mentioned earlier in this book, one of the most exciting things about real estate is that you can make as much money as you like, and if you are a good estate agent, you will make a good salary. I think I have made a good salary as an estate agent, but I have made far more money, and created far more wealth for myself, by buying and selling my own properties.

In my second book, *Buy Unlimited Investment Properties and Retire in 10 Years*, I described the different ways you can make money and create wealth from buying and selling real estate. Briefly, these are:

- Buy and sell real estate and make a profit from the sale.
- Buy real estate and hold or improve the property until you have sufficient equity to refinance. You can then draw on the equity and use it any way you like, including to live on.
- Buy and hold real estate, pay off the debt, and live off the rental income.

To find out more about these options, including other important topics such as how to improve your property to maximise capital growth, please refer to my second book, *Buy Unlimited Properties and Retire in 10 Years*.

To create a second, passive income, and wealth for

myself, I have used all the options mentioned above. Not only do these methods work, they are a lot easier and less stressful than going to work every day to chase another commission.

I am not trying to dissuade you from turning up at work tomorrow. What I would like to see every real estate agent do is get the most out of their career and make more money and wealth for themselves. As an estate agent, you have incredible opportunities to do this.

We know all the hard work it takes to be a successful agent: the dedication, the communication, interpersonal, and time-management skills, the attention to detail, databases, follow-up, and the long hours. But it doesn't take any skills to be a landlord. To become a successful estate agent, you need to learn your craft and hone your skills. This can take years. But it takes no time at all to become a successful landlord. The rental manager who looks after your investment properties does all the work for you. Occasionally, you will be asked to make a decision about accepting a tenant, reviewing the rent, or carrying out a repair on your property, but this is rare, and usually quick and easy. It doesn't take years to work out if you should increase the rent, and a rental manager is there to guide you through anything that might be tricky.

Any job where your salary is largely or entirely derived from commission or bonuses comes with inherent stress. If you don't make sales, you don't make commission. That could mean you can't afford next month's rent or mortgage repayment. You might have to miss out on certain luxuries, or even essentials like food. Whether you admit to it or not, the pressure to constantly perform to make your wage can be stressful and, after a time, tiring. If you are one of those highly ambitious agents who becomes the owner of a real estate agency, don't think that it will automatically become easier and you'll be able to coast through life with no stresses while earning lots of money. Of course, there are many very successful and profitable real estate agencies around, but each one faces its own challenges from time to time, and sales and money are not guaranteed month after month. It takes a great deal of effort not only to remain solvent, but to make a profit. All businesses must be run efficiently and skilfully to remain successful.

As I have mentioned, it is far easier to be a landlord than it is to be a successful real estate agent or business owner. For one thing, as a landlord I have never gotten a phone call from one of my tenants saying they feel sick and won't pay the rent that week, and nor have I received a call from a tenant saying they are on vacation for a few weeks and won't bother paying the rent while they are not living in my property. But I have received calls like this from employees, to say they are sick or taking a vacation and won't be in to make money for the business.

Unlike commission-based pay, your rental income is fixed and can be counted on month after month. In case something goes wrong, like your tenant stops paying rent or does a runner in the middle of the night and leaves the property with rent owing or, worse, in a damaged condition, there are insurance policies which cover these situations. You can also seek compensation through legislation and the tenant's bond.

I explained earlier that the more money we make, the more we spend. Of course, your salary is essential to live on, and to make a salary you need to work. Hopefully, we do not go to work just to sustain ourselves, but also to enjoy some of life's luxuries. If you buy investment properties, you will not need to go without luxuries.

I have shown that an estate agent who is an expert in their local real estate market can do all of the following:

- Identify what makes a good investment property.
- Find good investment properties that need minimal upkeep.
- Find "nicks"—properties that are for sale below their true intrinsic market value.
- Source good tenants.
- Manage their investment to the highest standard.
- Save on management fees charged by real estate agencies.
- Identify ways to increase rent, maximise the resale price of a property, and most importantly, create wealth for themselves by increasing their equity in the property.
- Save on selling costs (marketing fees and commission) if they decide to sell.

So, where to from here? If you already own an investment property, you are on your way to creating a second, passive income for yourself, which is commendable. If you haven't, and you want to know what to do next, this is exactly what you need to do:

1. Buy an investment property.
2. After 12–18 months, buy another investment property.
3. Repeat step 2.

In the rest of this chapter, I will explain exactly how to go through these steps.

Step 1: Buy an investment property

If you feel a little unsure about what attributes you should be looking for in an investment property, or you would like to see what attributes I personally look for, I cover these topics in detail in my first two books, *How to Buy Unlimited Investment Properties* and *Buy Unlimited Investment Properties and Retire in 10 Years*. But I will give you the essentials here.

When it comes to finding a property at a great price, don't doubt your own abilities. It would take the average investor months, if not years, of extensive research to gain the same knowledge of the local real estate market that you accumulate by going to work each day. You hone your knowledge every time you look at a property or research another sale result. You have carried out your due diligence and are ready to buy a property without further preparation.

Remember, though, you are human, and like anyone who has bought something very expensive, it is natural to wonder if you have paid too much. Buyer's remorse is a real condition that estate agents see frequently in their clients. It is normal to have these feelings, but through your work you are better placed than any other buyer to find those "nicks" we know are out there. If anyone can have confidence in their purchases, it's you; there is no need to be troubled by remorse if you use your knowledge.

It is crucial that you buy any property at the right price, particularly if you are going to sell it after just a short period (a couple of years or less). When you sell in that scenario, most of your profit will come from the price you paid for the property, not the sale price, which the market will determine.

Now, as step 1, buy an investment property within the next three months. You need to set a time limit. Make this commitment right now! Believe in yourself: you are ready. This is not an unrealistic timeframe; you do not need to buy a property by the end of business tomorrow. Three months is enough time to find a "nick". If you procrastinate and make excuses, you will most likely keep waiting for years. Don't make excuses; don't procrastinate any longer. This is the first step to your financial freedom. Whatever today's date is, add three months. When you find a suitable property, **buy it**.

If you are nervous or uncertain about your financial capacity to buy a property, make sure that you include a "subject to bank finance" clause in the sale contract. As you know, this will prevent you from buying a property at auction, because under the terms of an auction, all offers must be unconditional. The subject to bank finance clause is your ultimate safety net. If you have overcommitted and cannot afford the property, the bank will reject your loan application, and the contract you have signed to buy the property will not bind you. The other benefit of the subject to bank finance clause is that as part of the approval process, the bank will independently assess the value of the property you want to buy. This is usually done by a sworn valuer on behalf of the bank. The valuation will also give you peace of mind, because if the property you are buying is valued at less than the price you have offered, the loan will be declined.

If you buy a property within the next three months, you are on your way. I congratulate you. If you try to buy an investment property and fail because the bank would not provide you with finance, I suggest you look at the experience as practice for your next attempt. You will do better next time. Remember that you are infinitely better off having tried to do something and failed than if you tried to do nothing and succeeded. If you tried and failed, you are closer to succeeding next time. Again, if you are nervous about your ability to afford an investment property, make sure you include the subject to bank finance clause in the sale contract. Consider this absolutely non-negotiable: it *must* be included in the contract. This clause is your ultimate get-out-of-jail card if you have overcommitted and cannot afford to buy the property. Any money you have paid will be refunded, so the experience should not cost you anything other than your time.

Regardless of whether you succeed or fail in your first attempt to buy a property, within three months from now, you will have taken **action,** which is commendable. If you need further encouragement or help, ask people that already own investment properties, or contact me, I have included my details at the back of this book, and I would love to hear from readers about their experiences.

Step 2: After 12–18 months, buy another investment property

This may seem like an obvious step, but incredibly, many investors forget to do it.

I recommend that you wait 12–18 months before buying another investment property. For some investors, this may seem far too conservative—they may buy several investment properties in this timeframe. If you are a bit more cautious, the reason I suggest waiting 12–18 months is that, in most cases, it is enough time for the real estate market to have grown in value. After 12 months, you can get a new valuation for your property and show your bank how much your equity (wealth) has grown. This equity will help you buy another investment property.

Also, I have personally found that when you have owned an investment property for a while, the added activity in your bank account (rent money coming in and loan repayments going out) no longer seems strange. Once you get used to the extra activity, you will stop looking at your bank balance and worrying about the loan being serviced. You will realise the property is taking care of itself. At that point, you will be ready to buy your next investment property.

Step 3: Repeat step 2

If you follow this simple blueprint, in about 10 years you will most likely own six or seven investment properties. If we assume the average value of each property is between $300,000 and $500,000, your investment portfolio will be worth between $1,800,000 and $3,500,000. In about 10 years, this value will double. What you do then is up to you. But isn't it nice to have options?

I mentioned earlier that I followed a traditional career path in real estate. I began as a sales consultant and ultimately, I owned my own real estate office. I also mentioned that I made more money from investment properties than I did from making sales or owning my own agency, and this is precisely why.

Buying investment properties does not require above average intelligence or a lot of work. Anyone can do it. It just takes a conscious effort to buy your investment property, and then you multiply the effect by repeating that effort every 12–18 months to create a portfolio. After you have bought your investment properties, time becomes your friend. The longer you own them, the longer they have to grow in value. As estate agents, we have seen this. Just think back to properties you have sold in the past and consider what they are worth.

If you own an investment portfolio worth $10 million, in 10 years' time it will most likely be worth about $20 million. That means that you have made the equivalent of $1 million per year. You may think that is a ridiculous example, because you will never own a $10 million portfolio, but consider that in today's market the median house price in many capital cities and surrounding suburbs is already $1 million and rising. To have a portfolio worth $10 million may only require 10 properties. This is achievable. Of course, you may work in an area where the median house price is lower than $1 million, but owning a $10 million property portfolio now requires less properties than it did 10 years ago, and it will require even fewer properties in another 10 years from now.

Whether you are an estate agent or the owner of an agency, you need to work incredibly hard to earn $1 million per year. It will take enormous effort on your part, and years to hone your skills and build up your clients. You will most likely not do this in your first or second year, and in fact, you may never earn that much money in a single year. Likewise, when you start your investment portfolio, you are not going to earn $1 million per year in your first or second year. You need to build up your portfolio over many years. We understand that to be a successful real estate agent takes a great deal of work and dedication. If you only put a small fraction of that effort into building a property portfolio for yourself, you will probably find that in a few years, your investment portfolio could be making you as much or more money than your salary, with far less effort.

8

BE A LEADER

As an estate agent, you are probably very generous in giving your time to clients, particularly if you think there is a commission about to be made. But what about your work colleagues? We can become so focused on our day-to-day activities and targets that we forget to ask our colleagues how they are going.

In every office, as in life, some people want to be leaders, or are natural-born leaders, and others are happy to be led. You might fall into the latter category. But being a leader doesn't mean you need to have the loudest voice, make the most sales, or manage the largest rental portfolio. You can become a leader in your office just by being a positive influence.

You can lead by setting an example. You can lead by buying investment properties, building a portfolio, and showing your colleagues how they can do the same. And you can become a better leader by simply showing a genuine interest in your workmates. If you show an interest in your colleagues, they will usually share information with you and open up about themselves. This small gesture can have a profound and powerful impact on your relationship with them, and on the dynamic within the office.

Many surveys have shown salary plays only a small role in a person's job satisfaction. Other elements of that satisfaction include being part of a team, being acknowledged for good work, friendships within the office, and management taking an interest in staff. If you build your own investment portfolio and help others do likewise, you will help create a better office culture, which will lead to greater job satisfaction.

The best way to build a better office culture is by being inclusive. If you are going to run an **investment seminar**, run one in the office first, just for your work colleagues. This will give them the first opportunity to hear about the topics you want to cover in the seminar before you convey your knowledge to the public. It will also give you a chance to settle your nerves about public speaking, and to fine-tune your presentation. Most importantly, you can get invaluable feedback from your colleagues, who may share ideas and perspectives that you would never have thought of. This is to be expected, because everyone sees things differently. Something that seems perfectly reasonable or logical to you may not to someone else, and you need to make sure that you communicate your knowledge in a way that everyone can understand. All feedback is valuable and will help you create a better experience for the people who attend your seminars.

If you want to form **investment groups** like those I described in chapter 5, it is crucial that you first invite your colleagues to join the group. Whether or not they take up the opportunity, they will be grateful that they were offered it before anyone else. They may not have any interest in buying investment properties, but even so, if you do not invite them they could be resentful. If you invite them and they decline, they will still appreciate the opportunity.

Similarly, if you are going to hold information evenings

inviting people to join an investment group, first hold a session for your colleagues. You will receive the same valuable feedback as I described above in relation to investment seminars, helping you to plan and execute a better public event.

A further benefit of including work colleagues in your information seminars is that their comments and feedback, and their engagement with your ideas about investing, may lead you to new opportunities that you wouldn't have considered otherwise. Just like the real estate agencies they work for, most real estate agents have a rather narrow view of what they do: list and sell real estate or list and manage other people's rental properties. But in my opinion, one of the most exciting recent developments in the industry has been the emergence of buyer's advocates. In the not-too-distant past, the idea of these services would have been considered fanciful. Now, estate agents can receive commissions and fees for buying properties, bidding at an auction, appraising a property, and a whole host of other services—all performed on behalf of a client. By sharing information and ideas with your colleagues, and including them in your information nights and seminars, you may open new and exciting opportunities to build your business and your salary, which your colleagues can participate in.

If any of your colleagues want to join your investment group, I believe you should give them a special, reduced commission rate. For the reasons I explained earlier, you still need to charge a commission for your services, but do apply a reduced rate for your colleagues. Even if none of them join your investment group, they will know that they have been given an opportunity before anyone else and at a privileged commission rate. If your colleagues join your investment group, it will help build even more credibility with other investors. After all, if you are securing properties that are good enough for you, your work colleagues, and potentially your family and friends, there is a good chance that these properties will also be good enough for them.

Even if your colleagues don't join your investment group at first, you should still keep them informed of your progress. Every time you update the investors in the group, update your work colleagues as well. This is as simple as copying them in on all the emails and correspondence you send to your group of buyers.

You should do this not only because your colleagues might join the investment group later, but also because it makes them feel included and helps build a better team environment. Despite them not personally buying any investment properties with you, they may still be interested in knowing how your group is going, and they can still learn from your progress.

If you make your work colleagues feel included and special, you will build a better and happier office. Even if you don't consider yourself a natural leader, your colleagues will start to view you as one if you help create a better office culture.

PART II

THE REAL ESTATE AGENCY

Real estate is an uncompromising, cutthroat business, because it is all about the numbers—of sales, listings, phone calls, and client appointments you make. These numbers are everywhere, in black and white, and they don't lie or play favourites. If you don't make the numbers, you won't make it in the industry.

Real estate is not an industry that rewards your staff or your business for a good try. There is no prize for coming second. You either get the listing and make a sale (or rent a property) or you do not. The winner takes all the commission and second place gets nothing. Real estate is also highly competitive, with lots of agents and agencies chasing the next listing and the next sale.

If you own a real estate agency, you are very familiar with all these numbers and the pressures involved in reaching them. You know what each sales consultant and rental manager must do to be successful, and, most importantly, you understand what they need to do to make your business profitable. As an owner, you have most likely experienced both sides of the business. You probably started as a fresh-faced, naïve real estate agent, and over the years you gained experience, made some money, and ultimately bought or started your own agency. Because of your years of experience, you can understand the pressures estate agents face, and you give your staff all the tools they need to become successful. You want nothing more than for your staff to be successful, because the more successful they are, the more successful your business is. This may sound cynical, but it is an incontrovertible fact: without successful staff, your agency simply cannot flourish, and will not reach its full potential.

Each month, when the profit and loss statements are prepared, your eyes dart straight to the bottom of the page to see if you have made a profit for that month. If you are making money, life is wonderful. Life becomes more wonderful the more money you make, so it is understandable that so much focus and effort is put into achieving the right numbers. Without them, your business wouldn't exist.

Although it would be wrong to think that money is the only important motivating factor for your staff as they come to work each day, it is also understandable why you would think so. After all, if your business is making money, you are happy. If you are happy making money, then obviously your staff should be happy about making money as a reward for all their hard work. However, as I explain in the next chapter, money is not the most important factor in retaining and motivating staff. More staff quit their jobs because of a lack of opportunities (31%) than to chase a higher salary (6%).

As a business owner, your main focus and concern will always be on maintaining a profitable business and hopefully growing those profits each year. In the following chapters, I discuss different ways you can increase your bottom line, but always remember that unless you are the only one working in your business, you don't have a business without your staff. You need to stay vigilant about retaining all your good staff, as well as about making money. One can't happen without the other.

Clearly, there are many benefits for the real estate *agent* if they own a portfolio, but there are also numerous benefits for the real estate *agency* if staff buy investment properties. In the following chapters, I explain exactly why all real estate business owners should encourage their staff to buy investment properties and build portfolios.

9
STAFF RETENTION

There are many theories about the type of people you should look for when you are considering employing new staff, particularly in the sales and rental departments of real estate agencies. Some argue that you should employ younger people, because they are more enthusiastic and willing to do prospecting activities, while others urge you to employ more mature people because they build better trust and rapport with clients. Some believe you should stack the office with staff and let the strongest survive while the weakest perish, and others suggest hiring people with large debts because they are more highly motivated to make money. Still others suggest employing women, because they develop better, longer-lasting relationships with female clients and women make most of the decisions when it comes to real estate.

Why real estate agencies have high staff turnover

No matter which theory you subscribe to, one fact remains:

real estate has a high employee attrition rate. This is widely known and, unfortunately, well-accepted. As a result, in many agencies there is a belief that staff will only be there for a short time, and managers are continuously looking for new staff to cater to this turnover.

In the United States, 48% of realtors have worked for two years or less at their present agency.
The median tenure for all agents is four years.
(Information sourced from the National Association of Realtors 2017 Member Profile. Unfortunately, this information is not available for real estate agents in Australia, but I suspect the results would be like those in America.)

You may not think that staff turnover is all that high where you work, but think back over the last couple of years and consider all the staff, particularly sales staff, who no longer work in the industry. These people may not have been employed by your agency—they may have worked for your competitors—but think back to all those people who once had a profile in the local paper and on local real estate websites, who after only a short period no longer work in real estate. You will probably find the number sobering. It can be astonishing how many people, in just a couple of short years, start a new career in real estate, then disappear just as quickly as they arrived and are never heard of again.

Whether this sounds like your office or not, one thing is absolutely true: it's a huge pain in the backside for any office when a good employee leaves. It takes a lot of time and effort to train staff, which comes at a financial cost to the business. There is nothing more frustrating than an employee leaving after you have invested time and resources into training them, just when they have finally learned all the idiosyncrasies of your business and are starting to become a productive (and profitable) member of staff.

Unfortunately, this occurs far too often, and it is the bane of all businesses, particularly small ones that find it difficult to allocate the money and resources needed to fully train new staff. So it should be a goal of all businesses to create an office culture that rewards all staff and has a long-term perspective on staff retention. This is often easier said than done, because the real estate industry generally focuses more on the individual rather than the team, and on short-term performance rather than long-term career development. If each individual does their job and hits their targets, then collectively the whole office makes it. When this happens, it is important that the whole office celebrates the success as a team. This is particularly true for administrative staff, who usually do not receive bonuses or commissions, unlike sales consultants and rental managers, but are instrumental in contributing to the overall success of the business.

Most, if not all, business owners are aware of the importance of keeping good staff, and as a result many managers and business owners undertake management courses, which are often very costly, to learn how to retain staff. Nevertheless, staff attrition remains a very real concern for many real estate agencies.

Because real estate focuses so much on the numbers, which ultimately all lead to answering one question—did we make money or not?—we could believe that money is the main force that dictates our happiness and that of our staff. But despite what many people may think, salary is not the main reason people quit their jobs. The top seven reasons why people change jobs are shown below:

Lack of opportunities to use skills and abilities	31%
Bad management	22%
Toxic workplace or company culture	12%
Promotion	8%
Excessive or too little work	6%
Higher salary and financial stability	6%
Lack of rewards and benefits	4%
Other reasons	11%

(Source: Jan Tegze, "The 7 Reasons Why People Change Jobs", Recruiting Daily, 14 July 2017, https://recruitingdaily.com/7-big-reasons-people-change-jobs/.)

Many surveys like this have been carried out in the past, and all the results I have seen tell a similar story: salary alone is not enough to keep staff happy and retain them for the long term. Of course, giving a staff member a pay rise will make them happy for a short time, but if they are unhappy for any of the reasons listed above, a pay rise is only a quick fix that will not last forever. Other factors, such as those listed above, will negatively affect the workplace and any pay rises will be quickly forgotten.

As you can see from the results above, the top three reasons people quit their job—a lack of opportunities, bad management, and toxic workplace—account for the overwhelming majority (65%) of cases where people quit their job. By contrast, people only quit their job for a higher salary in 6% of cases.

According to the research, when people can put their skills and abilities to use in their jobs, they tend to feel a greater sense of self-confidence and accomplishment.

Employees are happier when they are engaged in activities they are good at, and which exercise their skills and abilities.

Employees want to develop their skills, and if a job doesn't give them the ability to do that, it will lead to dissatisfaction and they will start looking elsewhere.

Bad management and company culture are often intertwined, and both are cited as a major reason for employees quitting their job. Usually, managers are appointed to a position because they have the technical skills needed to perform the tasks they are responsible for overseeing. But this can be a mistake, because a manager is in a leadership role and may lack the interpersonal skills needed for the job. There are many facets to being a good leader, and one component is showing genuine interest in your staff and their well-being.

Taking a longer-term view will help you keep good staff

As an estate agent, I have worked in different real estate agencies and was previously a part-owner of my own real estate agency. I understand the intense pressure on employees and employers to make the next sale and keep the monthly commissions coming in. I can understand why we focus so much on immediate short-term goals that we often forget or even totally ignore longer-term goals.

Early in my real estate career, I had a short-term view of what I needed to do to be a successful agent and make my monthly commission. But as soon as I started actively investing in real estate, my focus changed, and I gained a much wider view of what I could accomplish in my career and what our real estate agency as a whole could accomplish. I went from thinking only about what was happening this month to also thinking about next year, the year after that, and beyond.

Once I took a long-term view of my career and my business, I believe I became a much better estate agent. When making decisions, I looked beyond the current month and took a much longer-term view of the goals I set for myself and my business. This change in my thinking made me more productive, motivated, content, and happy. Some of the stresses we face constantly as estate agents were alleviated because I knew I was building something much bigger and longer-lasting than just one month's commission.

If your staff begin buying investment properties, they feel a greater sense of self-confidence and accomplishment from putting their skills and abilities to use. They will be happier in their job because they are building something important for the future of themselves and their family. They will remain focused on reaching next month's KPIs and making next month's commissions, because they realise their wage lets them build their investment portfolio and wealth. This will ensure they remain highly motivated and productive. If they are highly motivated, they are more likely to stay, which builds their longevity in the business and, over time, their loyalty to it.

If your staff start buying investment properties, you show a genuine interest in their plans for the future, and you help them by encouraging them to buy more properties, which will enable them to achieve more wealth and independence, they will be far happier, more grateful, and more productive as employees. Showing an interest in the well-being of your staff is no guarantee that you will not lose some in the future, but it is a huge step to overcoming most reasons why staff quit.

One last note—one day it may be in your best interests to help your staff become wealthier. Sometime in the future, you will decide to sell your business. You cannot keep working forever, and the time will inevitably come when you decide to put your feet up and retire. When this time comes, who better to approach about buying your successful, well-established business then your loyal employees? If you have a successful, profitable business made up of happy staff, the buyer you are looking for may already be working for you.

10

ATTRACT BETTER STAFF

The bane of all businesses is losing good staff, and one of the dreaded consequences is that you need to start conducting job interviews to find new people. This is usually time-consuming and tedious work, which most people dread. When the time comes to sit down with the eager-eyed, hopeful new candidates, most senior staff members conveniently become too busy taking phone calls or meeting with clients to avoid sitting in on the interview. Even if you are in the fortunate position of looking for new staff because your business is growing and expanding, job interviews are still viewed with a great deal of reluctance. Obviously, they are important and necessary, and finding the perfect employee is essential for a harmonious, happy, and profitable business. Unfortunately, though, finding the perfect employee can be very difficult.

In an ideal world, instead of looking for the perfect employee, they would come looking for you. If you have a nice office with good staff that all get along, why shouldn't they? Your office is busy, but it has the right balance of work and fun. Why wouldn't people want to work there?

Even more thought-provoking, though—why would anyone want to leave?

What attracts staff to a real estate agency?

In attracting new staff, part of the problem could be that outside of your office, no one knows what a great place it is to work. If this is the case, you need happy staff that will tell others how great it is to work for you. Happy staff will be your greatest asset when it comes to attracting new people to your business. If you create the right work environment, this is possible. The best advocates for your business are the people working in it now. Your staff members know a wide and diverse group of people. This includes their family and friends, but may also include tradespeople, suppliers, and even your competitors. Through work or social networks, your staff may know people who work in other real estate agencies, or they may know people who would like to work in the real estate industry. Your staff will speak with these people about their own experiences working real estate, and more importantly about working in your office. As a result, your staff can be a great resource in attracting new staff—or they can be a deterrent to anyone considering a job with your agency.

We like to think our staff love coming to work. Within the office they may seem happy and content, but what do they say about their job satisfaction in private, or when the boss isn't listening? It is impossible to know exactly what people say behind our backs, but we would like to think that their private thoughts about work are also largely positive, because having happy staff has many benefits, including that it helps attract new staff.

Naturally, you will have happier staff if you create an office culture where you take an interest in their well-being, help them prosper in their job, and help them grow their wealth outside of work. When your staff are speaking with their friends, family, and acquaintances, they will let them know that you look after your employees and have helped them build their wealth by encouraging them to buy investment properties. This is very attractive to anyone considering joining your business.

Attracting the best estate agents can be hard. Typically, the very best agents look to join the very best agencies. Unless you are the very best agency, you might consistently miss out on employing the cream of the crop. Your attempts to attract the best and most experienced estate agents are like those of a football team trying to attract the best and most experienced players. The best performers in any industry can choose where they want to go. Football players want to go to the best team and try to win a premiership. The best real estate agents want to go to the best-performing real estate agency. They know there may be more staff in the best-performing agency, but are prepared to put their abilities to work in a competitive office environment. They go to the best agency because it has the biggest ads and the largest market share, and they believe that the more successful the office is, the more opportunities they will have to make money. Unless you are the best real estate agency in your area, you will struggle to attract the best-performing estate agents.

When you are trying to attract a proven performer, you need to ask yourself, what you can offer them. What makes your business better than the rest? Why would someone want to work for you? Importantly, what is your point of difference?

Keep good staff by supporting them in becoming investors

If yours is not the biggest and best real estate agency in the area, these can be confronting questions. You may already have had a proven performer from your office leave you to go and work for your opposition. Unless you offer something special, you will always be vulnerable to competitors poaching your best staff. When we are busy, and our office and its staff are all making money, we will tend to forget or even ignore the potential threat that people may leave. We become complacent and think it won't happen to us. It's only after a staff member leaves, and their name appears in our competitor's newspaper ad the following week, that we chastise ourselves and wonder what we could have done to hang onto them.

We may then start to become paranoid that one staff member leaving could lead to others leaving, and that we may have a mass exodus on our hands. This may not happen, but unfortunately, even one star employee leaving your business can have a big impact on the harmony and ultimately the profitability of your office. Imagine the fallout for your business if two or three staff members left at a similar time. You may think this is unlikely to happen, but I have seen a number of instances where groups of staff have left a real estate agency only to start up their own down the road or in the next suburb. To prevent this from happening, many employers now ask employees to sign a restriction-of-trade agreement when they commence employment. In my opinion, though, this has little power to stop staff from leaving one real estate agency and then starting at a different agency a short time later.

To help protect yourself from having staff poached by other real estate offices, and to attract the very best real estate agents to your business, you need to have a clear and attractive point of difference from all your competitors. I believe the most effective way to keep your staff and attract new people is to encourage them to become property-investment millionaires.

This does not mean every staff member has to become a millionaire immediately, or at the same time. Each staff member can start their own property-investing path whenever they like, and they can buy investment properties as quickly or as slowly as they like, but you will be there to encourage and help them. Imagine how powerful your job offer to new employees would be if you could say with complete confidence, "Join my real estate agency and I can help you become a multimillionaire with a large portfolio within 10 years." Not only would people be beating down your door to join your agency, they would also stay longer, because they would start with the belief that they will be with you for the next 10 years.

You might think this is overselling, and that you would be building up the new employee's expectations too high and setting them up for failure. You won't be. Don't *guarantee* that you will turn someone into a multimillionaire, because in the end it is up to the individual. You will not be doing the hard work for them, and in the end, you cannot *make* them buy investment properties. So there is a risk that they will not follow the plan, and not achieve the result.

But you *will* show them how to do it, and you will help them along the way. The best way to show them is to lead by example. You are the business owner and mentor, and hopefully their friend and confidant. When you buy investment properties yourself, you are showing them what is possible. After you have helped your current staff members buy investment properties and create financial wealth, you can use their stories to attract new staff.

Focus on investing to build a strong office culture

Initially, you may only have one or two staff members who are excited about buying investment properties and building portfolios, but in time, others will take an interest in what those staff members are doing. They will ask questions, and eventually they will try and emulate what their colleagues are achieving.

Staff who are actively investing will help others to do the same. They will work together to find and secure investment properties. This is not just limited to finding properties at the right price; it will carry over to all facets of the transaction, such as conveyancing fees, bank fees, and so on. Everyone in your office will take an interest in what is going on, and anyone in your office can join in at any time. This will foster greater camaraderie.

A way to involve all your staff in this activity is to run investment seminars and form investment buying groups, as discussed earlier. The first buying group you form may be entirely made up of your staff. As the principal of the business, you are in the best position to start such a group. This is a great way for you and your staff to form a stronger bond, helping all of you to become wealthier and making for a happier workplace. By creating stronger bonds and friendships in the office, you will make it far less likely that staff will leave to join your competitors. Competitors will still try to poach them, but when they are speaking with their friends, family, and acquaintances, they will be sure to tell them what a fantastic office they work in.

If you develop an office culture like this, you will keep staff for longer and attract the very best estate agents to your business. Estate agents from other offices will find out what your office is doing for its staff, and this will be a powerful incentive for them to consider joining your business. Any real estate agency can give a new employee a desk, phone, and receptionist. But you can give them a lot more than this. You have a clear and very powerful point of difference. You can help them make money in their work and outside of work, and by helping them plan for their financial future, you can back your claim to care about the well-being of your staff with concrete and powerful action.

11

GREATER SYNERGY

A typical real estate agency consists of a sales department, a property-management department, and an administrative department. The sales department and property-management department have regular meetings, at least once a week, and the administration department meets less frequently. Despite all these meetings, it is extremely rare for staff from one department to attend the meeting of another. Each department mostly works autonomously. The administration department has an overview of what goes on in the office as a whole, but staff from each department rarely have an in-depth knowledge of what their co-workers do.

But if a sales consultant buys an investment property, they will take a keen interest in the property-management department.

If a property manager buys an investment property, they will take a keen interest in the sales department.

And if a member of your admin staff buys an investment property, they will take a keen interest in both the sales and property-management departments.

It is in the best interest of everyone in the office to know what is going on in the real estate market as a whole and how that translates to what is happening in your agency. Are property prices going up or down? Are rents going up or down? What is happening in your business? A staff member's interest in how another department is performing may be born out of their own self-interest, but it helps build up their real estate knowledge. That will help them deal with clients, and builds greater synergy between your staff and the different departments of your agency.

A sales consultant may have in-depth knowledge of sale prices in the local area, and may be extremely confident in their ability to answer questions about buying or selling property. But when it comes to rental expectations and tenant profiles, they will go to the experts and ask for help from your property managers. Likewise, a property manager may know everything there is to know about managing a rental property, but when they think of buying one, they will seek advice and help from the sales team. This is to be expected, and it should be encouraged, because if your staff help each other, it will create a better office culture.

Usually, staff are so focused on their day-to-day activities that they take little or no interest in what is happening in the department next to them. A sales consultant is so focused on making the next sale that they have no idea what the current vacancy rate is in your office or how long it takes to find a tenant for a property. Equally, a property manager is so focused on the next ingoing condition report that they don't know what the auction clearance rate is in your office.

The attitude of your staff would profoundly shift if they started buying investment properties. Suddenly, your sales consultants will want to know how long it takes to find a tenant for a property, and your property managers will want to know if sale prices in the area are going up or down.

This new interest in all things real estate will open

conversations between staff that previously would not have occurred, and it will promote a better understanding of how each department operates and how it contributes to the success of your agency. It will foster friendships, and staff will be far more understanding and willing to help each other.

From time to time, all workplaces face the absence of a staff member due to illness, holiday leave, etc. Whether the absence is planned or unexpected, it always seems to happen when your office is at its busiest. If there is greater synergy in your office and your staff have a better understanding of what each department does, they can help one another when required. If a property manager is away, a sales consultant can meet prospective tenants at a property inspection. If a sales consultant is away, a property manager can meet a building inspector at a property for sale. At the moment, you may have staff who are reluctant to help other departments because they do not see it as their responsibility. This attitude would change if better friendships were formed within the office and each department took an interest in what the others were doing.

That synergy can be particularly useful if staff from different departments can help each other when someone leaves your agency or a staff member is away on an extended break like maternity leave or long-service leave. An understanding of each staff member's role is vital when there simply are not enough hands on deck in one department.

Encouraging greater synergy in your office is crucial. Not only is it a great catalyst for better harmony between staff, but it can also be a lifesaver when the unexpected happens, as it often does, and you need everyone working together as one united team.

12

GROW YOUR RENT ROLL

Most real estate agencies have a rent roll—a list of rental properties under management—and they work extremely hard to maintain and grow it. This is understandable, because the rent roll is an extremely valuable asset. One day, the owner of the real estate agency will retire, and most of the business's sale value is tied up in the rent roll.

To determine the value of a real estate business, you calculate the annual fees generated from the rent roll and then apply a multiplier, which will usually range between 2× and 2.75×. There may be some value assigned to other items such as plant and machinery, or less tangible items such as goodwill, but unquestionably, most of a real estate agency's value is found in the rent roll. Because of this, a business owner will usually take a keen interest in growing this asset. In a lot of instances, the rent roll is the owner's golden parachute into retirement, their nest egg.

Rent rolls can be, and often are, sold from one real estate agency to another. Buying a rent roll is a quick and effective way of growing the number of rental properties your agency manages, but for a number of reasons, it is best to grow your rent roll organically. Landlords that come to your agency because they were sold to you as part of a rent roll do not have any allegiance to you or your agency. They do not have a relationship with your property manager or staff. They did not ask to move their important investment property to your agency to be managed. These landlords were sent to you as a commodity, sold by a real estate agency that wanted to make some money, most likely because the owner is retiring. These landlords will not hesitate to leave your agency and give their investment property to your competitor if your agency does one little thing wrong or does not perform at the highest standard at all times. Fortunately, if you have a good property manager or managers, and they do the right thing in looking after these new landlords, the vast majority will usually remain with your agency. When you have good property managers, buying a new rent roll usually sees the landlords make a smooth transition from the old agency to the new.

Of course, if a new landlord comes willingly to your agency and you grow your rent roll organically, there is also no guarantee they will stay with you forever. If your property managers don't give them excellent service, they can leave your agency just as easily as a landlord you acquired through buying a rent roll. However, when a landlord chooses to sign up with your agency, they are less likely to leave at the first sign of something going wrong. Landlords that come to your agency willingly usually do so because they have been referred to you because of your agency's reputation, or because they have some rapport or relationship with one of your property managers or another member of your staff. These landlords are more likely to stay with your agency because they already chose you above other agencies for a reason, and as a result they are far more loyal.

Growing your rent roll organically can be a very slow process. It is very unlikely that one day you will arrive at work and find 20 new landlords waiting to give you their rental property to manage; growing your roll takes patience and commitment. Over time, more and more landlords will come to you because they have heard about the service your agency provides, and because your sales consultants are selling investment properties to investors who are introduced to your rental department. But regardless of how quickly or slowly your rent roll grows, you will persevere, because you know one day, when you are ready to sell, it will be worth a handsome amount of money. This is what drives all owners of real estate agencies that have a rent roll.

Now imagine if you could easily grow your rent roll with extremely loyal landlords. If every staff member in your agency bought one investment property and your agency managed them, how many new rental properties would your business have? How many more would you have if each person bought two investment properties? Obviously, the more staff you have, the bigger this number is going to be. But the number doesn't just relate to the staff working in your office. If every staff member started buying investment properties, they would naturally tell their family and friends about the properties they were buying. This would encourage those people to start thinking about their own investment plan and what they were doing about their financial future. Some of these people would also start buying investment properties, and likewise, they would give your agency the property to manage. The number of people would grow exponentially.

Of course, not every staff member is going to buy an investment property tomorrow, and if they do, probably not all of their family and friends are immediately going to buy an investment property, either. But when you are growing your rent roll organically, it is all about planting seeds and letting them grow. Initially, it may only be one staff member that buys an investment property, so you only get one new property to manage, but once the idea takes hold, it will only need time to flourish.

To help your staff and give them the best opportunity to create wealth and plan for their financial future, you should offer them and their immediate families lower management fees. How much you reduce your standard fees is entirely up to you, but they will be grateful for whatever discount you give them. They know that if they move their investment property to another real estate agency, it will cost them money. They will have to pay higher management fees, which will affect their cash flow and lifestyle. Also, by continuing to work in your agency they can keep an eye on how their investment property is being managed. This is a double win for the staff member—reduced costs and the ability to keep a close eye on their very important investment. Just like a landlord who chooses to give you their investment property to manage, a staff member who enjoys reduced management fees is not guaranteed to keep the management of their property with you forever, but it certainly increases your chances considerably.

13

PROPERTY EXPERTS

We have already discussed how employees and employers depend on each other. To own a truly great and successful real estate agency, you must have great staff working for you. Preferably, you would have some superstars among them. But equally, it is much easier for an employee to be a superstar if the real estate agency they work for is already highly regarded and considered a leader in their area.

Your staff work hard to make your agency successful, and you want them to be successful, too. This is not just because it is in your financial interest, but because you like your staff—otherwise, they would not be working for you. Because you want your staff to do well, you give them lots of training and support. But unfortunately, almost all the training staff receive rehashes training methods and practices that have been around for decades. Apart from marketing—because the internet and other marketing tools are continuously evolving as people look for the most cutting-edge ways to advertise a property—real estate agents do the same thing year after year. This may largely be appropriate, because the art of selling a property has not significantly changed in living memory. Some legislation may be different, but the way we build rapport with clients, conduct property viewings, and so on, has not. So the tried and proven methods are still relevant, and taught to new and experienced staff alike. Naturally, some employees will excel and shine like stars, while many others will only glow dully.

To supercharge your employees' success, I believe you should encourage them to buy investment properties. When they have done so, you should celebrate it by letting others know. When one of your staff buys an investment property, you should let your clients know, because it shows that you have a local expert on staff who is actively buying investment properties in your area. Your staff member has honed their skills and used them to buy investment properties, and they may have built a property portfolio and become a multimillionaire, or be on their way to doing so.

There are many ways you can tactfully inform people about what your staff are achieving, such as sending newsletters to your landlords and your database of potential clients, or through social media. You don't need to shout it from the rooftop, but when you are sending out a newsletter or the like, you should mention that your staff member has bought an investment property and if anyone is thinking about property investment, they should speak with that person because they are a local property expert. This will help give your staff member a greater sense of pride and confidence, and encouragement to continue building on their success.

Remember that people love dealing with successful people. Ideally, your business would only be made up of successful people. All your staff would be multimillionaires and property experts. If this were the case, your agency would be overrun with new landlords, buyers, and vendors wanting to give their business to you.

Just because a staff member is successful, buys investment properties and builds wealth does not mean they are suddenly going to leave you and enjoy retirement on a beach in some exotic location. Once people have had a taste of success and are making lots of making money, they usually want more. And as I mentioned in part one, the more money people make, the more they spend. They want and need to make more money if they are going to continue buying investment properties. Unless you are extremely fortunate, buying an investment property usually comes with a big, shiny new mortgage. The need to keep up their cash flow will ensure that your staff remain focused and motivated. Making money and having success drives people and is addictive. If you help your staff make money and succeed, you will have highly motivated, grateful, and loyal employees.

Property experts make you the leader in your area

The main reason for wanting property experts in your office is that you want your agency to be the leader in your area. You want to be viewed as the agency of choice, with the best staff and the best reputation. You want to grow your business and attract more clients to your agency.

Imagine how much more powerful your next investment seminar would be if it were presented by staff who were actively investing in your area. These seminars would have a lot more relevance for the audience. The people attending would find them more informative and interesting, and most importantly they would have a higher regard for the presenters.

It would also be far easier to attract buyers to join an investment group if your staff were already part of it and personally investing in real estate. Buyers in the group will feel more comfortable and confident with an estate agent who has a proven track record of buying investment properties.

As with most things in life, the more you do something, the easier it becomes. Running investment seminars and forming investment groups is no exception. Once you have formed one investment group and succeeded at buying properties in bulk, the next group will be easier to form, and the one after that will be easier again. Of course, an exciting thing about investment groups for the individual agent and your business is that when properties are found for the group, you don't just make one commission; you can make several commissions at once.

The success of your staff ultimately leads to the success of your business. The two go hand in hand.

PART III

RULES TO REMEMBER

TOP 5 RULES FOR REAL ESTATE AGENTS TO REMEMBER

1. Trust yourself

You are the **expert**. You are a confident and capable estate agent who can accurately assess a property's value. So you are capable of identifying when a property is being sold below its true market value. As an estate agent, you frequently speak with a variety of people about property investing, and your clients seek your advice about investment properties because they trust your opinion. Now you need to show the same amount of trust in yourself as your clients do.

When you identify a "nick", don't second guess yourself or wonder what the owner's reasons are for selling. That the property is being sold for a low price doesn't necessarily mean that there is anything sinister going on, or that there is something wrong with the property. There could be a number of reasons why the owner needs to sell quickly, such as financial pressures, a matrimonial settlement, being transferred to work in a new city, a deceased-estate settlement, etc.

Remember, no one is in a better position than you to buy investment properties. You have an in-depth knowledge of your local area that is far superior to that of any other buyer. This puts you in the perfect position to identify the best properties to buy for the best possible price. You are the local real estate expert. You need to use your skills and knowledge for your own financial future and your family's future, rather than always giving away your knowledge freely to other property investors who take advantage of your expertise in planning for their financial freedom.

2. Be the local expert

To do this, you need to buy an investment property in your area and then you need to let others know. You do not have to be boastful or tell everyone you meet. When you buy an investment property, you will naturally tell your family and friends, and you will tell your work colleagues because your estate agency will look after the management of your property. This is a good start. In time, other people, such as landlords, other investors, and potential clients will discover that you are investing in the area.

These people will be interested to find out what sort of property or properties you have bought, if you are going to buy more, when you are going to buy them, what type of property you look for, and so on. You want people to know you are investing in the area because it is another tick on your resume. People already know you work in the area, and they may know you are a successful real estate agent, but you also want them to know you are spending your own hard-earned money to buy investment properties in the area. By putting into practice all those things you have told your clients in the past, you are proving that you are really the local expert, and that it is not just talk.

Remember that people like dealing with successful people, but they do not like dealing with arrogant people. If you are successful *and* humble, people will be attracted to you. As a result, you will have more clients, and in an industry where numbers mean everything, you will be a better and more successful agent.

3. Don't pigeonhole yourself

Estate agencies have a narrow view of what they do, but this is also true of estate agents. Don't think of yourself as just a sales consultant or property manager. Think of yourself as a real estate expert and, more importantly, start thinking of yourself as a property investor. Even if you haven't bought an investment property yet, start thinking about the property you are going to buy whenever you are looking on the internet or in real estate newspapers. Having this goal in mind will change your mindset and the way you look at properties.

When you look at real estate through different eyes, you will quickly realise there are opportunities everywhere. They are all around you. Every time you look at a property, you will start to wonder what sort of investment property it would be, what improvements you would make to attract higher rent, and what improvements could attract a better sale price. You will also be better able to help your clients with their real estate needs.

You will find opportunities to make money in so many different ways, in addition to the traditional ways you make money now. Every day you go to work will be exciting, and you will very quickly realise you are in the perfect position to take advantage of your job and skills. No other buyer, except maybe other estate agents working in your area, has the same in-depth local knowledge. Don't limit yourself—it is now time to take advantage of your position and create a passive income for yourself in the future.

4. Make more money

The aim of every person working in the real estate industry is to make as much money as possible. This is the nature of our industry, and of any other industry where salaries are entirely or largely derived from commissions or bonuses. It was likely one of the things that attracted you to real estate in the first place. Most estate agents are always trying to improve their skills and income, and the desire to earn lots of money drives most agents to work long hours.

Estate agents are given copious training in traditional ways to earn money by making sales and attracting rental listings. This training is imperative; it ensures that you understand the fundamentals and get the foundation you need to make a successful career out of real estate. Once the foundation has been laid and you are an estate agent, in time you will become a real estate expert, and then you should transition into being a property investor as well. The amount of time this metamorphosis takes will be different for every person, but it should be as natural as it is inevitable. If you are an estate agent, in time you will become a better estate agent, and in time you should use your skills to buy investment properties.

You can be an estate agent, a property expert, and a property investor all at the same time. One role does not distract from the others; in fact, they complement each other and enhance the credentials you present to your clients.

As your career grows, you need to look at new ways of making money, particularly in such a highly competitive industry as real estate. Even if you are already a superstar estate agent, remember that all stars eventually fade. You may be fortunate, and your star may shine brightly for a long time to come, but one day you may just want to stop working so hard and start spending more time relaxing with family and friends. Whatever the reason, when your star begins to lose some of its lustre, you will be grateful that you created a secondary, passive income for yourself and your family.

Earlier, I described investment groups and the numerous benefits of buying properties in bulk. With these groups, I was able to earn multiple commissions at once, but more importantly I was able to buy investment properties for myself at prices below their intrinsic market value. With the advent of buyer's advocates, there are now numerous ways an estate agent can earn a commission. I have mentioned a few of them, and there are now many exciting opportunities available to estate agents that previously were not available. When you are going about your normal day-to-day tasks, try to keep your mind open to new opportunities. If you are receptive to new ideas, you will realise there are opportunities to make money and create wealth all around you.

5. Lead by example

Leaders come in all shapes and sizes. There are dictators, totalitarian leaders, and benevolent leaders. Some leaders are loud, while others are softly spoken. I believe the best leaders are the *inclusive* ones, who get everyone involved and taking ownership of whatever they hope to achieve. By giving everyone ownership, inclusive leaders make everyone feel important and valuable. Each person is an essential part of the team, with a common goal.

This is easy to achieve; all it takes is communication. If you discuss things with your colleagues, they will feel part of what's going on, and if there is a problem, hopefully they will be part of the solution.

But it is just as easy to fail in this area. As humans, we have a keen desire to feel needed and wanted, but we can get caught up in our own activities and stop communicating with those around us. Then we become isolated. This can have disastrous consequences on our relationships with colleagues and with people outside of work.

As I have mentioned, everyone in the real estate industry wants to make as much money as possible. That's the main reason people choose to work in industries where pay is mostly driven by commissions or bonuses. You can be inclusive in your pursuit of wealth, too. If you are buying investment properties to create wealth for yourself, let your family, friends, and colleagues know how you are doing it. Don't brag or force your ideas and opinions onto others. Some people will have no interest in real estate; those people will not ask you about your experiences. However, others will be very interested in what you have achieved, and they will ask lots of questions.

Simply because you discuss what you are doing with other people, they will start to view you—and treat you—differently. In the vast majority of cases, they will respect your opinion more when it comes to real estate because you are putting into practice what you have learned and turning your knowledge into wealth through property investing. People will have a greater respect for you and in many cases may even be a little envious. They will start to view you as a leader, not because you are loud or brash, but because you have done something positive. Be inclusive, share your experiences with your work colleagues, and you will find it makes for a happier, more harmonious office.

TOP 5 RULES FOR REAL ESTATE AGENCIES TO REMEMBER

1. Encourage your staff

Encourage your staff to take advantage of every opportunity available to them while they are working in real estate. You have dedicated, hard-working staff. These people are the pillar of your agency's success. As a team, there is nothing in real estate they cannot do. They can accurately appraise the value of a property; negotiate with vendors, buyers, landlords, and tenants to achieve desired outcomes; identify good and not-so-good investment properties; find good tenants; maximise rental income and sale prices; and overcome unexpected problems. Collectively, they can handle any part of the real estate investment process.

Your staff look after their clients and their best interests. Now they need to look after each other's best interests as well. These motivations do not have to be in conflict, or mean that the service and attention to detail they are currently giving clients will suffer. It simply means they should not limit themselves to using their skills and knowledge only in looking after clients' needs. As a business owner, you should encourage your staff to work together as a cohesive team and help each other (and yourself) create wealth through investing in real estate.

If they do help each other, your staff will become an incredibly strong, happy, and united group of people. The synergy between your sales consultants, property managers, and administrative staff will grow, and your office will hum like a finely tuned Ferrari. If someone needs to jump into a different department to help, they won't hesitate. All the staff will take a much keener interest in all aspects of real estate, including how your agency is performing and how it can improve. They will want to know how everything is going at work, instead of thinking that is someone else's problem. Your staff will become more productive and learn more about themselves, each other, and real estate.

As I explained in chapter 9, "Staff Retention", people want to use their skills and abilities at work. I can't think of a better way your staff could use their skills and abilities than to buy investment properties for themselves. Unfortunately, as a business owner, there is nothing you can do to guarantee good staff will stay with you forever, but if you encourage them, take an interest in their well-being, and help them create wealth through property investing, you are far more likely to keep your staff for longer. This can also be a point of difference from your competitors, which will help you attract the top performers in the real estate industry.

2. Create an office of superstar property investors

Your superstar property investors will also be your local property experts. All new investors should be directed to these superstars, because they are the most qualified people to look after them. Obviously, your superstars can answer all the standard questions investors ask, like "How is the market performing?", but they can also give more in-depth information, such as why they personally invest in the area, what type of property they buy, what kind of tenants they attract, what they do to attract higher weekly rents, and so on.

Anyone who buys an investment property from your agency, or uses your agency to manage their investment property, will speak with family, friends, and **other investors** about their experiences with your company. Naturally, you would like your agency to be the first choice for any property investors in the area. If your agency has superstar estate agents that are also property investors, your reputation as the go-to agency will be enhanced. The property investors you have as clients will believe they are receiving a higher level of service and advice from these local experts. They are more likely to keep buying investment properties from you, and will refer more clients to your agency.

By directing all new investors to your superstar property-investor agents, you are effectively saying they are the best people to speak with about property investment, even if you don't say so directly.

Whatever industry we work in, or whatever job we do, we all want to be known as the best in our field—the person to go to. This is also true of your staff. Even if they don't appear outwardly competitive, they will secretly want to be the best and be acknowledged as the best. If you have superstars buying investment properties, creating wealth, and helping new investors do the same, other staff in your office will want to emulate them. Having an agency with superstars can be highly motivating.

3. Run investment seminars

As I have mentioned, many real estate agencies have run the occasional investment seminar in the past. Organising and running a seminar involves a lot of work, and unfortunately there are no guarantees that it will be a success. Typically, an agency holds one seminar and then forgets about doing another one until years later.

In an effort to keep landlords informed about what is going on in the real estate market, real estate agencies often send them a newsletter that goes out with the rent statements. We are typically good at committing to this as a regular exercise.

Running a regular investment seminar, conducted by your superstar property investors, is far more powerful than a monthly, quarterly, or annual newsletter, which often goes straight in the bin. The benefits for your agency are numerous. It gives you a chance to build better and stronger relationships with your current landlords and clients, it gives you a better chance of poaching some of your competitors' clients, and it establishes your agency and superstar property investors as the local experts. Seminars are an important opportunity to position your real estate agency in the marketplace. You want to be known as the local experts.

If you are running an investment seminar and have a superstar who is uncomfortable presenting in front of a crowd, or if you have only a small crowd, I suggest you abandon the podium and have your star sit in a comfortable armchair on stage (or in front of the audience). As the principal of the agency, you should sit next to them and have a chat just like you would in your office. To make the setting even more relaxed, you can position the armchairs around a small coffee table and have a pot plant or other decorations on display. The idea is to create an intimate setting which makes it feel less like you are putting on a big show and more like you are making the audience part of an exclusive club.

A comfortable setting will also be less intimidating for your staff. If you are having a friendly chat, your superstar doesn't need to look directly at the audience, in case that makes them nervous. It is also far easier for someone to answer questions than to prepare a formal presentation, and their responses may be more natural than a presentation would be. It's fantastic if you have more than one superstar: then you can have a panel of experts ready to discuss property investing and answer questions.

After you have finished having a chat, let the audience ask questions. If the audience is a smaller group of people, they won't feel daunted about asking questions, which can lead to a more in-depth and enlightening discussion. Hopefully, the audience will have lots of questions you may not have thought of, and the outcome will be an interesting seminar for everyone present, with lots of interaction.

Running investment seminars is also beneficial and motivating for staff who attend but are not presenting. They will learn more about property investing, and they are more likely to be inspired to one day buy their own investment properties. Even if they don't openly express a desire to one day be a superstar property investor, many will secretly harbour a desire to become one, and some may even aspire to present at a future investment seminar.

The most important thing about running investment seminars is not to give up after the first one. We know that in real estate, you need lots of perseverance. Running investment seminars is no different. The more you run, the easier and more successful they become. That your audience may be small should not be a deterrent. Holding a seminar with lots of people does not guarantee you will list more properties for sale, sell more properties, or gain more rental properties to manage. Sometimes, you can get better results from a smaller group of people. It's all about the quality of the seminar, rather than the quantity of people attending.

If you are thinking about running investment seminars, think about ways you can make them different from what other agencies are doing. What will make your seminar stand out? A panel of local experts from your agency seated on stage answering questions from your clients is a good start.

As I have mentioned, you need to run more than one seminar. In addition to the newsletters which you are currently sending out to your clients and landlords, I believe you should run an investment seminar about every six months. You can run them in your office if you have the space; this will make them easier to organise, keep costs to a minimum, and create a comfortable environment for your staff. Some of your clients may even be visiting your office for the first time, and this is an ideal opportunity to familiarise them with your business. Remember, you want to make the audience feel like they are a part of a special investment club. That way, they will keep coming back.

4. Form investment buyer groups

As I write this, I am not aware of any real estate agencies currently forming investment buyer groups. If you are one of the first to start, it will be an excellent point of difference from your competitors, and it is also a great way to earn multiple commissions at once.

Your real estate agency will have an extensive database of landlords, buyers currently looking for properties, and past buyers who have purchased from you. The current and past buyers are usually divided into "homebuyers" and "investors". Most agencies do nothing more with this list other than send out newsletters and Christmas cards.

Some client databases are enormous and will contain many hundreds of names and addresses. Such databases could be incredibly profitable if you used them to organise your clients into buying groups. Obviously, not all of these people will immediately jump at the chance of joining a group, and like all aspects of real estate, getting people on-board will take persistence. But every successful buying group you form will lead to more success. After all, who wouldn't like to buy properties at tens of thousands of dollars below market value?

Once you have successfully found properties for one buyer group, forming the next one will become easier and the one after that will be easier again. Your reputation for forming these groups will quickly grow, and new clients will contact you asking to join. This will happen because you are providing a unique service and each buying group comprises multiple buyers, multiplying your success and the referrals you will receive. These buyers will be your advocates and will recommend your agency to family and friends.

In addition to your current newsletters, you should also send out a newsletter that deals exclusively with the success of your buying groups. Again, when people learn about the properties you have bought and the savings made, finding new people to make up more groups will become easier and easier.

If you are thinking about forming buyer groups, running investment seminars is a great place to start. At the seminars, you will meet people who are eager to join your buyer groups. Attendees will obviously be interested in investing in real estate, and many of them will be actively searching the market at that moment, looking for their next investment property.

While the investment seminar is a great starting point, you should not do a hard sell at the seminar about forming these buyer groups. You could mention that your agency is about to offer an exciting new service that involves forming buyer groups, and explain a few of the benefits. But the investment seminar is all about meeting people, building up your database, and showing your agency's credentials. People attending the seminar will want useful information, but not a hard sell. If you try too hard to sell them on joining, they will be less inclined to attend your future seminars.

5. Continue to look for new and innovative ways of making money

We know real estate is already a very competitive industry. It is growing more competitive each day, with new real estate agencies opening regularly and "self-sell" real estate businesses proliferating. The big claim made by all the "self-sell" businesses is that they can give the property owner the marketing tools required to sell their own property and save thousands of dollars in commission. Whatever you think of these businesses, they are here to stay; new variations will keep popping up because there will always be a segment of the real estate market that they appeal to.

With all these competitors vying for a piece of your market share, it is incredibly important that you remain relevant and continue to grow your business. Otherwise, it will be overrun by the competition and gradually fade away, with ever-diminishing profits.

As I have said, real estate agencies tend to have a narrow view of what they do, and they have been doing the same thing for decades. Apart from new marketing techniques and technologies you may have adopted, what does your office do differently now compared with ten or even two years ago?

I know there has been an explosion of information, and that now reports provided to clients are more detailed and comprehensive than ever before, and filled with myriad graphs in all shapes and colours. But every real estate agency is providing these reports. Whenever there is a new tool developed for the real estate industry, such as valuation reports, video tours of properties, or light-up signboards on properties, all real estate agencies are quick to embrace them for fear of being left behind. As a result, very few agencies can boast a clear point of difference from their competitors.

Really, all real estate agencies do a very similar thing. To further illustrate my point, many years ago all real estate agencies used black-and-white sketches to advertise properties for sale; now they all use colour photographs. Previously, floor plans and aerial photographs were not provided for properties for sale; now there is a floor plan for every property, and there are aerial photographs for most, taken from a drone. This pattern is true for so many things in real estate.

All agencies embrace each new tool in the hope it will give them a point of difference. If you are one of the first real estate agencies to use a new technology, you will indeed have a point of difference—but it won't last long. Almost as quickly as you have printed advertising material about your new technology, your competitors are undergoing training on it and preparing to do exactly the same thing.

And without a clear point of difference, your business will always be vulnerable to competitors.

In my opinion, average, medium-sized real estate agencies are the most vulnerable, and are in constant danger of losing market share. I do not believe they have a clear point of difference, generally, and the public finds it difficult to differentiate between them. These agencies are profitable in good times, but when times get tough and sales become harder, as they inevitably do now and then, these agencies are most in peril.

However, I believe there will always be a place for

boutique real estate agencies that can micromanage their business and ensure they stringently control their overheads when times get tough. Boutique agencies that successfully manage costs in hard times can easily become cash cows in good times, when the real estate market and sales boom. These agencies offer their clients the personal touch they cannot find in larger agencies.

I also believe there will always be a place for the biggest real estate agencies, and that they will keep getting bigger. These agencies have the largest market share, the largest advertising campaigns, and consequently the highest brand recognition. Importantly, they also have economies of scale that lets them make larger profits, which insulate the business from disaster when times get tough and sales volumes shrink.

So, particularly if you are a medium-sized real estate agency, you need to keep looking for new innovative ways of making money. Here are two confronting and difficult questions you cannot ignore:

1. Do you have a strong point of difference?
2. Why should a homeowner give your agency their home to sell or manage rather than the agency down the street?

If, in answering these questions, you denigrate or belittle your competitors in any way, you lose. To correctly answer these questions, you must clearly show why your agency is the best choice. You should never win business by putting down your opposition; you should be better than your opposition. So answer the questions from a positive point of view: "We are better because…"

In my opinion, if you attack your opposition and point out their failings, you are also doing damage to the real estate industry as a whole. We all need to work together to lift the public's perception of our industry. Unfortunately, a lot of people do not hold estate agents in high esteem. If we tell them how bad other agents and agencies are, this will only reinforce any prejudices they already have.

If you have a truly unique point of difference, you will ride out the tough times, keep your staff, attract new people, and grow your business.

Coming up with new ideas is obviously not easy; if it were, everyone would be doing it. It involves thinking outside the square. Sometimes this is easier for people who are not working in the industry, because they look at things with a fresh set of eyes. It can be difficult if you work in the industry every day, because you are too close to it and too entrenched in doing things a certain way. As I have shown, a new idea today can be old news tomorrow, but to stay relevant and prosper you must be continuously looking for new ideas. Some of what you imagine may seem fanciful, but not so long ago, a virtual tour of a property would have seemed like pure fiction. Today it is a reality.

Obviously, I am particularly excited about the prospect of making money by forming buyer groups, but I also believe there is enormous scope to make money from all sorts of buyer-advocacy services, such as bidding at auction for buyers, valuing properties for them, and negotiating the purchase of properties on their behalf. In fact, I believe that buyer-advocacy services will continue to experience explosive growth in years to come. With property prices increasing and people finding it more and more difficult to get into the real estate market, I believe demand for buyer advocates will increase enormously.

Be open-minded to new opportunities, because they can come in all shapes and sizes. One day, you might include a conveyancing service as part of your business, offer formal sworn valuations, adopt a business model where you share profits with your staff, or venture into building properties and developments rather than just selling them. You may even be interested in listing your business on the stock exchange. No idea is too fanciful. Just because something hasn't been done before doesn't mean it is impossible.

CONCLUSION

What would you think of a mechanic who doesn't service their own car, a plumber who doesn't fix their own toilet, or a cleaner who gets someone else in to clean their home? Pretty silly?

How, then, do you think people view estate agents who don't buy investment properties? I don't think an estate agent buying real estate is any different from a stockbroker buying shares. It is a natural and understandable progression from their work experience, as they use their skills and knowledge to try and make more money. Every person older than 10 years of age knows the importance of having money and wants more of it. And if people are doing the right thing, acting legally and ethically, why shouldn't they use their skills and knowledge to make money?

Real estate agencies are very good at encouraging and training staff to make as much money as possible for the agency, but they unfortunately stop short of encouraging their staff to look at investing in real estate. In fact, the only time I have ever heard mention in a real estate office about staff buying investment properties, it was to inform staff of the policy that no staff member, and no member of their family, was permitted to buy a property listed for sale with the agency. That agency had made the policy despite legislation now existing (in the jurisdiction where I worked) to enable such transactions under certain conditions.

I suspect the agency's policy exists so it does not miss out on its commission. Under the legislation I mentioned, an estate agent can, under strenuous conditions, buy a property that is listed for sale with his or her real estate agency. The key condition is that in that case, the agency is *not* permitted to ask for commission or fees from the seller.

So, although staff and their family members may now buy properties listed for sale with their own estate agency, I believe the most prudent course of action for any real estate agency is still to discourage staff from buying properties from their agency. There is an enormous amount of property for sale in the marketplace and the risk, remote as it may be, of a backlash or bad publicity from one internal sale turning sour is not worth the possible gains. It is a case of risk versus reward. If you, or your staff and their families, buy properties listed for sale with other agencies, there simply is no risk of this kind.

Despite this caveat that it is best to avoid buying from your own agency, I strongly believe real estate agencies should encourage their staff to buy investment properties, and even train them on how to do it and what the benefits are. This training doesn't need to come at the start of a real estate agent's career, and it certainly shouldn't come before the new agent receives training on how to conduct a market appraisal or prospect for new listings.

Once the agent has established themselves, though, I believe they should receive training about investing in real estate. How long it takes for someone to become established in their job will come down to the individual. Naturally, some people will take longer than others, but in most cases, someone will be established in their job after about 12 months. Raising the issue of investing in real estate can be as simple as asking the agent during a staff review if they have thought about buying an investment property.

Some staff will be excited about the prospect of buying investment properties, while others will not have thought of it, being more concerned about which pub they will be drinking at on the weekend. Of course, there is no reason to subject any staff member to training on how to buy investment properties if they have no interest. But if you run these training sessions and staff within your agency start buying investment properties and building portfolios, even those staff who were not interested at first will still surreptitiously take note. They will realise that their colleagues and friends are planning for their financial future and your agency is helping them. Despite their overwhelming desire to party on, they will also want to be a part of what is going on in your office.

Most people know the saying "keeping up with the Joneses", and even if the partiers deny it, they will also want to keep up with their colleagues. Even if certain staff do not immediately jump on the idea of buying an investment property, they will know that any real estate agency offering this type of training and taking this kind of interest in its staff is a special place to work.

I believe there is a public perception that estate agents are flashy: they make and have lots of money, drive expensive cars, wear designer suits, talk fast, crack wise, and don't work too hard, because selling properties is easy. I also believe, thanks largely to the abundance of real estate shows currently on TV, that the general public thinks real estate is glamorous.

In most cases, the reality of what estate agents do and are is quite different from that image. In a lot of cases, real estate is a hard slog. The vast majority of estate agents work long hours, and often the reward is very little for the time and effort involved. People outside the industry often forget or ignore that most estate agents work entirely for commission, and unlike most workers, an estate agent is not guaranteed an income month after month. I believe that if estate agents everywhere started buying investment properties and building portfolios, the reality may begin to align with the perception that people have of estate agents. If many of the professional estate agents making up the real estate industry had large property portfolios and were millionaires, the industry would be even sexier and more glamorous, and many more people would choose to work in it.

My hope is that every real estate office starts taking an interest in its staff beyond what property they are going to sell or rent next. I hope they actively start training staff on how to buy investment properties and encourage them to do so. It is then my hope that staff start on their own paths to creating wealth through property investing.

I would like every real estate office to have at least a few millionaire property investors. The exact number, of course, may depend on the size of your office. These investors can then become the mentors and trainers for other staff in the office. As I have explained in this book, I believe the benefits for staff and the agency will be enormous.

APPENDIX: APARTMENT SALES TO THE BUYING GROUP

Appendix: Apartment sales to the buying group

Apt	Valuation	Sold Price	For Sale Price	Our Buy Price	Saving
1	$570,000	$570,000			
2	$550,000	$550,000			
3	$550,000	$550,000			
4	$550,000	$550,000			
5	$575,000	$560,000			
6	$540,000	$540,000			
7	$560,000	$560,000			
8	$556,000	$555,000			
9	$550,000	$550,000			
10	$570,000	$570,000			
11	$540,000	$540,000			
12	$540,000		$540,000	$512,607	$27,393
13	$540,000		$540,000	$512,607	$27,393
14	$545,000		$545,000	$517,357	$27,643
15	$540,000		$540,000	$512,607	$27,393
16	$576,000	$570,000			
17	$556,000	$555,000			
18	$561,000	$560,000			
19	$550,000	$550,000			
20	$561,000	$560,000			
21	$530,000		$530,000	$503,107	$26,893
22	$525,000		$525,000	$498,357	$26,643
23	$525,000	$525,000			
24	$525,000	$525,000			
25	$525,000		$525,000	$498,358	$26,642
26	$561,000	$560,000			
		TOTAL	$3,745,000	$3,555,000	$190,000

CONTACT THE AUTHOR

Thank you for reading my book. I hope that you found it interesting and thought-provoking, and that is a catalyst for change in the real estate industry, which I love.

I would love to hear from readers who want to discuss any topic mentioned in this book, or who have real estate stories they would like to share.

I promise I will reply to all readers who write to me, but please note that messages must be in English.

Please write to me at
markreister01@gmail.com

ABOUT THE AUTHOR

I have only ever told a few of my closest friends the whole story of why I wanted to start a career in real estate.

It started when I was selling a townhouse I owned in trendy South Perth, Western Australia, a street away from the Swan River and with views of the city skyline. My real estate agent was a young, gorgeous blonde woman with long legs, a short skirt, tailored jacket, designer sunglasses, and a tan that went on forever (possibly only in my imagination), who always drove her red MG convertible with the top down.

She was the reason I wanted to get into real estate.

She made the industry look glamorous and, just as importantly, she made it look easy. I listed my trendy townhouse for sale and within a few days, my estate agent showed an investor through. The investor quickly agreed to pay the full asking price and then, to everyone's surprise, made a further offer to buy all of the furnishings. My real estate agent concluded the entire sale faster than I could watch the *Lord of the Rings* trilogy, then drove out of my life with a very healthy commission cheque.

I share this story with you because in this book, I discuss people's perception of real estate agents. I believe most people see real estate as a sexy, glamorous, easy job that pays a lot. I was one of those people. But as I now know, and as most real estate agents know, other people's perception is often a world away from the reality.

Before I started my real estate career, I was working in a

clerical position for a large mining company. At that stage, I had never sold anything in my life. Fortunately, I had a natural aptitude for real estate, and in my first year after joining Woodards Real Estate in my home state of Victoria, I won their award for best first-year performance. That was in 1993. I went on to win many awards while employed at Woodards, including Victorian novice auctioneer of the year in 1998/99.

In 2002, I moved to Shepparton, a large country town in northern Victoria, and joined Rossignoli Real Estate, where I won numerous sales awards while following the Pilling System. I was the sales manager there for eight years before opening my own Professionals Real Estate office in 2010 with two business partners. Then, in 2014, as an adjunct to my core business, I started the Shepparton Buyer Advocacy Service.

I have written two books, *How to Buy Unlimited Investment Properties* and *Buy Unlimited Properties and Retire in 10 Years*, and have run numerous seminars to educate investors on the benefits of investing in real estate, particularly using the methods described in my first two books. I have also formed many successful buyer groups, which are described in this present book.

I left the Professionals and Shepparton Buyer Advocacy Service in 2016 to enjoy an early retirement. I had decided some years before that I wanted to retire at age 45. I worked in the real estate industry for 23 years. In that time, my love of real estate grew from a career into a passion. I love real estate, and I am thankful for the opportunities and lifestyle it has given me. I also love speaking with anyone who has a similar interest in real estate.

When I was a part-owner of my own real estate office, I had many titles: business owner, director, sales consultant, auctioneer, buyer's advocate, trainer, and author, and I was fully licenced. I am proud of the career I was able to make for myself, which culminated in business ownership, but since leaving the real estate industry, the title I am most proud of is property investor.

With the support of my wife, I have been able to create an investment portfolio for myself and my family that is in the top 0.9% of property investors in Australia. I don't mention this to be boastful or egotistical, but because I want to share my experience that creating that portfolio was far easier than any other accomplishment I achieved in my real estate career. I hope that this and my earlier books successfully communicate how and why I built my portfolio, and more importantly that they inspire others to forge their own path by buying investment properties.

Since finishing work in 2016, my interest in real estate has never waned. I still love looking through real estate newspapers and the windows of real estate agencies, particularly when I am on holidays and my wife is scouring the dress shops near an agent's office. I have never stopped loving real estate and following the industry.

I have also discovered I can't stay still for any extended period of time. Sure, I can sit and relax for a few hours, reading a book on a banana lounge by the side of a pool when the sun is shining. Who can't? But I am starting to look at my retirement as more of a sabbatical, because I need to have a project on the go, or else I go a little stir-crazy.

This book has been one of those projects, and I hope you have enjoyed it and that it inspires you. Now I will need to start thinking about what's next, so look out—you never know where I might pop up.

As a final note, when I was planning this book, I decided all the profits from its sale should go to the Fred Hollows Foundation (FHF). The FHF is a fantastic, independent not-for-profit organisation that does wonderful work here in my native Australia and more than 25 countries around the world, restoring sight to more than 2.5 million people. They are currently working towards eliminating avoidable blindness and improving the health of Indigenous Australians. A more detailed description of the work they do follows on the next page. On behalf of the FHF, I thank you for the contribution you have made by buying this book.

[f] facebook.com/mark.reister.3

THE FRED HOLLOWS FOUNDATION

The Fred Hollows Foundation today

Since its humble beginnings in Fred and Gabi's kitchen, The Foundation now works in more than 25 countries and has restored sight to over 2.5 million people.

The Foundation is driven by Fred's vision to eliminate avoidable blindness, for Indigenous Australians to have access to quality health services, and to stand up for what is right. It believes that collaboration, getting things done with integrity, and empowering local communities is the best way to make a difference.

Today, there are 36 million people in the world who are blind—but many don't need to be. The Foundation focuses on preventable and treatable diseases such as cataract, trachoma, and diabetic retinopathy. Its in-country work involves local training and providing affordable technology, so doctors, nurses and health care workers can recognise, diagnose, refer, and treat eye problems in their communities. It uses research to improve its understanding of avoidable blindness, then uses the findings to implement strategies and advocate for change.

Fred's influence

Fred was the type of man who knew exactly what he wanted, then went about getting it. Through his years with the Aboriginal Medical Service, the National Trachoma and Eye Health Program, and his work in developing countries, he was driven by the injustices he saw.

Being the man he was, he spent his final years planning to establish factories in Eritrea and Nepal and develop low-cost lenses in these two countries that he cared deeply about. Months before his death, he also flew to Vietnam to keep a promise to train ophthalmologists in modern eye-surgery techniques so that local people would be empowered to help their own communities.

The Foundation is working just as tirelessly as Fred did to end avoidable blindness—by fighting injustice, building local capacity, empowering the countries where it works, and staying true to its values. He had a big dream, and it's a dream that lives on in the work of The Foundation.

Together, we can do this

The Foundation knows exactly how to help mothers who are pulling out their eyelashes in agony from trachoma. It knows how to treat children who are needlessly blind from cataract and to get them back to school. It knows how to prevent people with diabetes going irreversibly blind because they can't access quality eye care.

The Foundation knows how to help, but there's a lot of work still to be done across the world and in Indigenous communities in Australia. Eliminating avoidable blindness can be achieved—with the help of The Foundation's partners and, most importantly, its invaluable supporters.

Please help keep Fred's vision alive by donating today at www.hollows.org

www.ingramcontent.com/pod-product-compliance
Lightning Source LLC
Chambersburg PA
CBHW020425220526
45464CB00002B/567